The Relationship Code For Couples

The Proven Guide to Solving Tension Building Openness, and Growing a Stronger Happier Relationship

Annabel Whitmore

Copyright © 2025 by Annabel Whitmore

All rights reserved.

No portion of this book may be reproduced in any form without written permission from the publisher or author, except as permitted by U.S. copyright law.

This publication is designed to provide accurate and authoritative information in regard to the subject matter covered. It is sold with the understanding that neither the author nor the publisher is engaged in rendering legal, investment, accounting or other professional services. While the publisher and author have used their best efforts in preparing this book, they make no representations or warranties with respect to the accuracy or completeness of the contents of this book and specifically disclaim any implied warranties of merchantability or fitness for a particular purpose. No warranty may be created or extended by sales representatives or written sales materials. The advice and strategies contained herein may not be suitable for your situation. You should consult with a professional when appropriate. Neither the publisher nor the author shall be liable for any loss of profit or any other commercial damages, including but not limited to special, incidental, consequential, personal, or other damages.

Book Cover by Red Squirrel Publishing

First edition 2025

Contents

Free Gift for You — V

Introduction — VI

1. Foundations of Effective Communication — 1
2. Active Listening Techniques — 7
3. Understanding and Managing Emotions — 15
4. Conflict Resolution — 21
5. Non-Verbal Communication — 28
6. Building and Rebuilding Trust — 36
7. Communication Styles and Adaptation — 46
8. Self-Reflection and Personal Growth — 55
9. Creating a Safe Space for Vulnerability — 63
10. Practical Exercises and Scenarios — 72
11. Apology and Forgiveness — 81
12. Empathy and Understanding — 90

13. Mindful Communication	98
14. Addressing Common Pain Points	108
15. Aligning Communication Styles	117
16. Progressive Communication Approaches	129
17. Overcoming Fear of Vulnerability	135
18. Long-term Communication Strategies	141
Conclusion	152
Resources	156
Citation List	157

A Special Gift Just for You

As a thank-you for choosing this book, we've included a free bonus gift to support your journey.

🎁 The Couples' Sunday Check-In

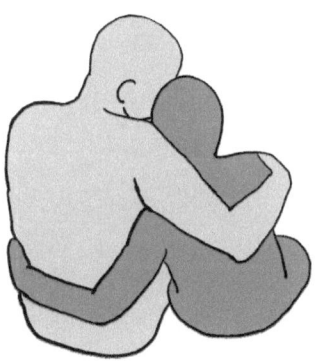

- Feel Closer in Just 10 Minutes a Week.
- No Deep Talks, No Therapy, No Pressure
- A gentle weekly ritual to reconnect, reflect, and reset together, even during the busiest seasons of life.

Click the link to claim your free gift: Here

Or Scan the QR code

Introduction

I wrote this book because I've been that person, the one sitting across from someone I love, feeling like we're speaking different languages.

During my first marriage, I remember a particular Sunday morning. We were both reading the paper, coffee getting cold between us, and I realized we hadn't had a proper conversation in days. Just logistics, who's picking up groceries, what time is dinner, did you pay the electric bill? I looked at this man I'd promised to spend my life with and felt like I was looking at a stranger. How had we gotten so good at living parallel lives under the same roof?

It wasn't the big fights that unraveled us. It was the slow fade of connection, the way we stopped really seeing each other. By the time we tried to fix it, we'd forgotten how to talk to each other without it feeling forced or awkward.

Maybe you know this feeling too. Have you ever been in the middle of what should be a simple conversation about weekend plans, only to find yourself in a full-blown argument about something completely different? Or felt like your partner just doesn't "get" you, no matter how many times you try to explain? My favourite expression at the time was "you're missing the point".

If so, you're not alone. In my sixty-three years, through two marriages, a few cringeworthy relationships, countless friendships, and observing people around me, from my own children to couples I've met traveling the world, I've learned that most of us never learned how to communicate. We just winged it and hoped for the best.

This book is the guide I wish I'd had decades ago. It's everything I've learned about what works, not from textbooks, but from real life. Because we finally learned how to communicate, my second marriage is flourishing. (it's not perfect, but getting better). Witnessing my friends' journeys through new love to empty nest syndrome… From late-night conversations with strangers on cruise ships who opened up about their deepest relationship struggles.

You'll find their stories throughout these pages, actual couples who shared their communication wins and struggles with me. These aren't perfect people with perfect relationships. They're ordinary couples figuring it out as they go, just like you and me. Some have been together for five years, others fifty. Some are still learning to trust each other; others are rediscovering intimacy after decades together.

What I've discovered is that successful communication isn't about being perfect or never fighting. It's about showing up, listening with your whole heart, and choosing a connection over being right. It's about the small, daily moments that either build bridges or create distance.

My husband and I laugh about texting each other from different rooms to ask who's putting the kettle on, but we also know when to put the phones down and look at each other. We've learned that the quality of our conversations shapes the quality of our life together.

This book will meet you wherever you are, whether you are newlyweds learning each other's rhythms or long-term partners wanting to reconnect. Whether you're navigating your first serious relationship or trying to rebuild after betrayal. Whether communication feels hard or you just want to make good, even better.

Together, we'll explore what it means to express yourself, to listen not just with your ears but with your heart, and to build the relationship that deepens rather than dulls.

Let's create the love story you've always dreamed of, one honest conversation at a time.

Just a quick note: I'm not a trained therapist, just someone with life experience, a lot of curiosity, and a deep interest in how relationships work.

Foundations of Effective Communication

I'll never forget the morning I finally saw the invisible load I'd been carrying. It was a Saturday, and there I was juggling breakfast, a basket of laundry, and the grocery list that lived permanently in my head. My husband sat at the kitchen table, reading his book with his coffee still warm.

That's when it hit me like a slap: I'd somehow become the manager of our entire emotional world without either of us noticing.

I was the one remembering his mother's birthday, smoothing over tension when his work stress spilled into our evenings, and always, always being the first to apologize after any disagreement. Not because I was wrong, but because I couldn't stand the silence.

This invisible workload has a name: emotional labor. And if you're reading this, chances are you know exactly what I'm talking about.

The Weight of the Invisible

Emotional labor is all the behind-the-scenes work that keeps relationships running smoothly. It's anticipating your partner's needs before they voice them, managing the mood of the household, and carrying the mental load of everything from social obligations to family dynamics.

During my first marriage, I remember feeling like I was the relationship's emotional air traffic controller, constantly monitoring and adjusting to keep everything flowing. I'd sense when he was having a tough day and shift my mood to compensate. I'd plan our social life around his energy levels, remember which topics to avoid when he was stressed, and somehow ended up being responsible for both of our happiness.

The tricky thing about emotional labor is that it often emerges naturally. But over time, what begins as caring can become overwhelming if it's not shared.

I've watched this pattern play out in so many relationships. There's always one partner who becomes the emotional barometer, the one who notices when something's off and tries to fix it. The other partner often has no idea how much mental energy this takes because it's invisible to them.

One of my dearest friends, Sarah, once told me she felt like she was carrying a backpack full of rocks that only she could see. Her husband would ask why she seemed stressed, confused, while she was mentally juggling his work deadline, their daughter's school project, his mother's upcoming visit, and that they hadn't had a proper conversation in weeks.

Sharing the Load

The solution isn't to stop caring or to create a rigid scorecard of who does what. It's about awareness and intentional sharing.

In my current marriage, we learned to discuss this invisible work. We made a list once, writing all the emotional and mental tasks that keep our relationship healthy. Things like:

- Initiating tough conversations

- Remembering important dates and events

- Managing family relationships

- Planning our social life

- Checking in on each other's emotional state

- Being the peacekeeper after disagreements

Seeing it all written was eye-opening for both of us. We realized how much I'd been carrying without either of us recognizing it.

Now we check in regularly. If I notice I'm feeling overwhelmed by the emotional management, I can say something like, "I'm feeling like I'm doing all the emotional heavy lifting this week. Can we talk about how to balance this better?" It's not about blame; it's about partnership.

Speaking Each Other's Language

Here's something I learned the hard way: you can love someone and still completely miss the mark on making them feel loved.

In my first marriage, I showed love by doing things, acts of service. I'd pack his lunch, organize his workspace, handle all the household details that made his life easier. I thought I was loving him well. Meanwhile, he showed love through physical affection, always reaching for my hand or giving surprise hugs.

The problem? I needed words of affirmation. I needed to hear that I was appreciated, that I was doing a good job, that I mattered to him. And he needed quality time, just us, without distractions or my endless to-do lists running through my head.

We were both giving love, but neither of us felt truly loved. It was like he was speaking French and I was speaking Spanish, both beautiful languages, but we couldn't understand each other.

Dr. Gary Chapman's concept of love languages finally gave us a framework to understand this disconnect. The five languages are words of affirmation, acts of service, receiving gifts, quality time, and physical touch.

My friend Maria figured this out before I did. She realized her husband felt most loved when she sat with him in the evenings doing nothing else, just being present. Meanwhile, she felt most loved when he helped with household tasks without being asked. Once they understood this about each other, their whole dynamic shifted.

The beautiful thing about love languages is that they're not static. My current husband and I discovered that my need for words of affirmation has grown stronger over the years, while his need for quality time has become more important, as we've gotten busier with life.

We make it a point to check in about this regularly. "What's making you feel most loved lately?" is a question that appears in our conversations more often than you might expect.

Building Trust One Conversation at a Time

Trust isn't built in grand gestures. It's built in Tuesday morning conversations over coffee, in the way you listen when your partner mentions something small that matters to them, in showing up consistently even when life gets chaotic.

I used to think trust was about the big things, fidelity, and honesty. And those things do matter. But I've learned that daily trust is built in much smaller moments.

My husband and I have a strict "no phones at the table" rule that has transformed our relationship. It seems simple, yet it revolutionized how we relate to each other. Before this rule, we'd sit across from each other, both scrolling, occasionally making surface-level comments about our days. We were together but not really connected.

Now our dinner conversations range from silly observations about our day to deeper talks about dreams, worries, and everything in between. Some nights we laugh until our sides hurt. Other nights we work through something that's been bothering one of us. The phone rule created space for trust to grow because it showed we were prioritizing each other.

Consistent communication is like watering a plant. Miss a day here and there, and it's fine. But go weeks without genuine connection, and something withers.

I see this with couples all the time. They love each other, but they've fallen into parallel lives. They discuss logistics, schedules, practical matters, but they stop sharing their inner worlds. Then one day they look at each other and realize they're living with a stranger.

The antidote is intentional, regular connection. It doesn't have to be deep every time. Sometimes it's just, "How are you feeling about that meeting tomorrow?" or "What was the best part of your day?" These small threads of connection weave together to create a sound foundation of trust.

Trust grows when your partner knows they can count on you to be emotionally present, not just physically, in the same room. It grows when you remember what they tell you about their worries and check in later. It grows when you create space for them, to be honest, without fear of judgment or criticism.

Building this kind of trust takes time, but it's the most valuable investment you can make in your relationship. Because when life throws you curveballs, and it will, you'll have a communication foundation strong enough to handle whatever comes your way.

To complement this chapter, the following resources are available to download at the end of the book.

- **The five languages of love.**

Active Listening Techniques

I'm sitting across from my daughter last year, nodding enthusiastically while she tells me about some drama at work. I'm making all the right sounds, "mmm-hmm," "oh really?", but inside my head I'm planning dinner, wondering if I remembered to pay the electric bill, and thinking about that conversation I need to have with my neighbor about her dog.

Then she stops mid-sentence and says, "Mom, you're not really listening, are you?"

Caught red-handed. And embarrassed, because here I was, someone who's spent years learning about communication, and I was doing exactly what drives me crazy when others do it to me.

That moment was a wake-up call. There's a world of difference between hearing someone and actually listening to them.

The Art of Listening

We all think we're good listeners. After all, we have ears, don't we? But true listening is something entirely different. It's like the difference between having music playing in the background while you cook versus sitting down with your favorite album absorbing every note, every lyric, every pause.

I learned this lesson during my first marriage. My ex-husband would come home from work, clearly needing to decompress, and I'd ask about his day while simultaneously folding laundry, checking my phone, and mentally organizing the next day's schedule. I thought I was being efficient, handling multiple things at once.

What I was doing was sending the message that whatever he had to say wasn't important enough for my full attention. No wonder our conversations became more surface-level. Why would he share anything meaningful when I was clearly only half-present?

Active listening means putting everything else aside and concentrating on what the other person is saying. It's about engaging not just your ears, but your heart and mind too.

My friend Janet discovered this when her teenage son started giving her one-word answers to everything. She realized that she'd been asking "How was school?" while checking emails, making dinner, or sorting mail. The moment she started sitting down, making eye contact, and waiting for his response, their conversations began to change. It wasn't immediate, but gradually he started sharing more, first just details about his day, then eventually opening up about friendship drama, worries about tests, and his dreams for the future.

The Power of Reflecting Back

One of the most powerful listening tools I've learned is paraphrasing what someone has just told you. It sounds simple, but it's revolutionary.

When my current husband says, "I'm feeling really stressed about this project deadline," instead of jumping to solutions or reassurances, I try to reflect back what I'm hearing: "It sounds like you're feeling a lot of pressure with this timeline, and it's weighing on you."

This does two things. First, it shows him that I actually heard what he said. Second, it gives him a chance to clarify or add more detail. Sometimes he'll say, "Yes, exactly, and I'm also worried that..." Other times he might correct me: "It's not so much the deadline, it's that I don't think the project is heading in the right direction."

Either way, we're having a proper conversation instead of me guessing what he needs or making assumptions about his feelings.

I watched my sister master this with her husband during a difficult time when he was dealing with job loss. Instead of rushing to fix his feelings or offer advice, she would reflect back what she was hearing: "You're feeling uncertain about the future," or "This whole situation is making you question your worth." He later told her that feeling truly heard during that time got him through it.

Getting Out of Your Own Head

The biggest barrier to good listening? Your own mind. I'm notorious for this. Someone talks, and immediately my brain formulates responses, thinking of similar experiences I've had, or jumping ahead to solutions.

During a heated discussion with my daughter a few months ago about her career choices, I caught myself mentally preparing my counterarguments while she was still explaining her perspective. I had to stop myself and say, "Wait, let me actually listen to what you're saying instead of preparing my defense."

That pause changed everything. When I really listened, I realized her concerns weren't what I thought they were. She wasn't asking for my advice or approval; she was asking for my support and trust in her judgment.

External distractions are easier to control than internal ones. Put the phone in another room. Turn off the TV. Clear the clutter from the conversation space. But managing that internal chatter? That takes practice.

One technique that's helped me is something I call "parking lot thinking." When my mind wanders or prepares responses, I mentally "park" those thoughts to come back to later. I tell myself, "I'll think about dinner after this conversation," or "I'll plan my response after I hear everything they have to say."

Real Listening in Action

Let me share a story about Andrew and Kara, a couple I met during my research. They've been married several years and have learned something valuable about communication that many couples miss.

Andrew & Kara's Story:

> Andrew (33) and Kara (32) from the USA have been married for several years, and for communication, they say they're "really on the same page." Their answers reflect a thoughtful, evolving relationship where both partners are learning, adjusting, and continuing to choose connection even when things get challenging.

> They feel heard when they talk and feel safe being emotionally vulnerable with each other. While they only occasionally talk about emotional needs directly, they've developed a rhythm that works for them. Disagreements are handled with care, sometimes one of them withdraws, sometimes they take space, and sometimes they talk things through after cooling off.

One thing that helps them feel close is what Kara calls "meta conversations", moments when they step back from daily life and reflect on how things are going overall. "We re-stock, talk through worries, concerns, joys, or frustrations, and feel some healing at the end," she shared. It's this reflective practice that helps them reconnect and reset.

Their communication styles differ slightly, Kara avoids conflict, while Andrew is more direct. That difference can be a source of miscommunication. Kara admits that she sometimes assumes she's done something wrong and can misinterpret Andrew's directness as frustration. When that happens, she can become defensive or withdraw.

They've explored love languages and use them, which helps bridge some of those gaps. What works best, they say, is carving out time to talk, especially when they know something's bothering the other person. It's not always easy to open up, but they've learned that it's worth it.

While they haven't had a single big breakthrough, they've seen their communication evolve. As Kara puts it, "We may frustrate each other more than at the beginning, but we've also learned how to talk those moments through, apologize when we're short, and share our concerns more directly."

Their advice to other couples is thoughtful: "It's not about winning or losing. Communication shouldn't be a competition. It's about coming together as a unit to figure out how rough points can be smoothed out, for everyone involved."

My thoughts:

Andrew and Kara have figured out something crucial: communication is a skill that evolves. They're honest about their different styles and the challenges that creates, but they keep working at it. Their "meta conversations" are genius, stepping back from the day-to-day to check in with each other.

Reflection Prompt:

What does "coming together as a unit" look like in your relationship? Are there moments where your goal becomes proving a point instead of understanding each other, and how could that shift?

Creating Space for Understanding

Here's something I wish I'd understood earlier in life: empathy and sympathy are completely different things, and mixing them up can actually create distance in your relationships.

I learned this the hard way when my best friend was going through a divorce. Every time she shared her pain, I'd respond with sympathy: "Oh, that's awful," or "I'm so sorry you're going through this." While well-meaning, I wa, putting myself above her situation, looking down with pity.

What she needed was empathy, for me to step into her experience and sit with her in that difficult space. Instead of "That's terrible," she needed to hear, "This must feel incredibly overwhelming," or "I can see how hurt and angry you are."

The difference? Sympathy says, "I feel bad for you." Empathy says, "I'm here with you in this."

Creating an empathetic space starts with intention. When my husband and I have our weekly check-ins (yes, we schedule them, it's the only way they happen consistently), we begin by saying something like, "I want to understand where you're at right now." That simple statement sets the tone for everything that follows.

We've also learned to establish some ground rules: no phones, no interrupting, no jumping to solutions. Just listening, understanding, and reflecting back what we're hearing.

I remember one evening when my husband was struggling with a difficult decision about his aging father. Instead of offering advice or reassurance, I tried to mirror what I was hearing: "It sounds like you're torn between wanting to respect his independence and worrying about his safety."

He paused, then said, "Yes, exactly. And I feel guilty no matter what I choose." That's when I knew we were having a real conversation, not just an exchange of information.

The Ripple Effect

When you practice empathetic listening, something beautiful happens in your relationship. Conversations become deeper. Trust grows stronger. Both people feel safer being vulnerable because they know they'll be met with understanding, not judgment or immediate solutions.

My daughter commented recently that she feels more comfortable talking to me about difficult things now than she ever has. When I asked why, she said, "Because I know you'll actually listen instead of immediately trying to fix me or the situation."

That feedback meant the world to me, because it told me I'd finally learned to offer what I'd always wanted to give: a safe space for the people I love to be completely honest about their experiences.

Empathy isn't just a communication technique. It's a way of showing up in your relationships that says, "Your feelings matter. Your experience is valid. I'm here with you, not to fix or judge, but to understand."

And that, more than any advice or solution you could offer, is often what the people you love need most.

To complement this chapter, the following resources are available to download at the end of the book.

- **Active Listening Exercise**

Understanding and Managing Emotions

The first time my ex-husband raised his voice during an argument, my whole body went rigid. Not because I was afraid of him, but because suddenly I was eight years old again, hiding in my bedroom while my parents screamed at each other downstairs.

That's the thing about emotional triggers—they don't care that you're a grown adult who knows better. In that moment, I wasn't a woman in her thirties trying to work through a disagreement with her spouse. I was a scared little girl who had learned that raised voices meant someone was about to get hurt.

It took me years to understand that my intense reaction to conflict had nothing to do with the present moment and everything to do with old wounds I'd never healed.

When the Past Hijacks the Present

We all have those buttons that, when pressed, send us straight into emotional chaos. It's criticism, for some people. For others, it's feeling ignored or dismissed. For me, it was conflict itself, any sign of tension and I'd either shut down completely or become overly accommodating, desperate to restore peace at any cost.

I remember one particularly ridiculous fight with my first husband about whose turn it was to take out the garbage. What started as a simple logistical conversation somehow escalated into me sobbing and him storming out of the house. Looking back, it had nothing to do with trash and everything to do with my deep-seated fear that any disagreement meant our relationship was doomed.

My friend Linda has a different trigger. If her husband doesn't respond to her texts quickly enough, she spirals into panic, convinced he's losing interest in their marriage. It sounds irrational until you learn that her first serious boyfriend used to give her the silent treatment as punishment, sometimes for days at a time. Now, any silence feels like abandonment, even when her husband is in a meeting.

These triggers are like emotional land mines buried in our psyche. We step on one, and suddenly we're not responding to what's actually happening, we're responding to what happened years ago.

Recognizing Your Pattern

The first step in managing triggers is recognizing you have them. This sounds obvious, but it's not always easy. When you're in the middle of an emotional reaction, it feels justified and rational.

I started keeping what I called an "explosion journal", not the most flattering name, but it was accurate. Every time I had an outsized emotional reaction to something, I'd write down what happened, what I felt, and what the situation reminded me of.

The patterns became obvious pretty quickly. Anytime I felt criticized or judged, I'd become defensive and argumentative. Anytime there was tension in the air, I'd start frantically trying to fix things, even when they weren't really broken. And anytime I felt ignored or overlooked, I'd either withdraw or become attention-seeking.

Seeing it all written down was both embarrassing and enlightening. I realized that most of my relationship problems weren't about the present, they were about ghosts from my past that I'd never dealt with.

Learning to Pause

Once you recognize your triggers, you can start learning to manage them. This doesn't mean you'll never get triggered again. I still do, regularly. But you can learn to pause before you react.

My current husband and I have developed what we call the "time-out signal." If either of us notices we're getting emotionally flooded, we can call a time-out. No explanation needed, no judgment. We just step away for a few minutes to calm down before continuing the conversation.

The first time I used it, I felt silly. We were discussing our budget, and I felt overwhelmed and defensive when he questioned one of our expenses. Instead of snapping at him or shutting down, I said, "I need a time-out. I'll be back in ten minutes."

I went to our bedroom, did some deep breathing, and asked myself what was really going on. I realized his question had triggered my old fear of being controlled, something that had nothing to do with him or our current situation. When I came back, I could explain what I'd felt and why, and we had a productive conversation instead of a fight.

The Wisdom of Emotional Intelligence

Here's something I wish I'd understood in my twenties: emotions aren't the enemy. They're information. The goal isn't to stop feeling things; it's to understand what your feelings are trying to tell you and respond thoughtfully instead of reactive.

I learned this lesson when my daughter was a teenager and we were constantly butting heads. Every conversation seemed to end in slammed doors and hurt feelings. I kept focusing on her behavior, trying to get her to be less dramatic, less emotional, less... teenage.

Then my sister pointed out something that changed everything: "Maybe stop trying to fix her feelings and start trying to understand them."

So I started listening differently. Instead of hearing her anger and getting defensive, I tried to hear the hurt underneath it. Instead of dismissing her frustration as melodrama, I tried to see the world through her eyes—a world where everything felt overwhelming and adults seemed to have all the power.

The shift was remarkable. Once she felt heard and understood, the intensity of her emotions didn't disappear, but the way she expressed them changed. Our relationship transformed because I'd learned to respond to her emotional state instead of just reacting to her words.

Carrying Yesterday's Hurt into Today's Love

We all come into relationships carrying invisible baggage from our past. Some of it's heavy, betrayal, abuse, abandonment. Some of it's lighter but still limiting, like learning that love comes with conditions or that conflict means the end of safety.

During my first marriage, I had no idea how much my childhood was influencing my adult relationship. I'd grown up in a house where emotions were either suppressed or explosive, where love felt conditional on good behavior, and where conflict was something to be avoided at all costs.

So I brought all of that into my marriage without realizing it. I became a people-pleaser, desperate to keep the peace. I suppressed my own needs to avoid any possibility of conflict. And when problems arose, I had no tools for working through them because I'd never learned that two people could disagree and still love each other.

It wasn't until that marriage ended and I started to reflect, that I understood how much my past was dictating my present. I had to learn, at thirty-eight years old, that it was okay to have needs, okay to express dissatisfaction, and okay to work through problems instead of just avoiding them.

Rewriting Your Story

Healing from emotional baggage doesn't mean forgetting your past or pretending it didn't shape you. It means recognizing the patterns that no longer serve you and choosing different responses.

My breakthrough moment came during a conversation with my current husband about something trivial—where to go for dinner. I found myself getting anxious because I could tell he had a preference but wasn't stating it directly. In my past, unstated preferences led to passive-aggressive behavior and resentment.

But instead of falling into my old pattern of frantically trying to guess what he wanted, I simply asked: "It seems like you have a preference. What sounds good to you?"

He looked surprised and said, "I was hoping for Italian, but I'm fine with whatever you want."

That was it. No hidden agenda, no trap, no test. Just honest communication about dinner preferences. It was such a small moment, but it showed me how much I'd changed. I was no longer automatically assuming the worst or responding to threats that didn't exist.

The Journey Continues

Working through emotional baggage and learning to manage triggers is ongoing work. There's no finish line where you suddenly become perfectly emotionally regulated. But every time you choose awareness over reaction, understanding over assumption, you're building new patterns that serve you better.

My relationship now feels fundamentally different from my first marriage, not because my husband is perfect or because we never have conflict, but because we've both learned to respond to what's actually happening instead of what we fear might be happening.

The emotional intelligence and self-awareness I've developed has rippled out into every area of my life. I'm a better mother, a better friend, and definitely a better partner because I've learned to pause, breathe, and ask myself: "What's really going on here? What am I feeling, and why?"

It's not always easy, and I don't always get it right. But the work is worth it, because on the other side of understanding your emotional patterns is the freedom to choose different ones. And that freedom opens up possibilities for connection and intimacy that I never knew were possible.

To complement this chapter, the following resources are available to download at the end of the book.

- **5-4-3-2-1 grounding exercise.**
- **Emotional trigger reflection exercise.**
- **Gratitude Journal.**

Conflict Resolution

Last month, my husband and I had what I call our "great dishwasher debate." It started as a simple question about whether dishes needed to be rinsed before going in the machine and somehow escalated into a discussion about household standards, childhood upbringings, and whether one of us cared more about cleanliness than the other.

Twenty minutes in, we both started laughing because we realized we were having a passionate argument about soap residue.

But here's the thing - that ridiculous fight brought us closer together. Once we stopped defending our dishwasher philosophies and started listening to each other, we discovered something important. It wasn't about the dishes at all. He was feeling like his contributions around the house weren't being appreciated, and I was feeling overwhelmed by the mental load of managing household details.

The dishwasher was just the messenger.

When Fighting Leads to Understanding

I used to think conflict was the enemy of good relationships. Growing up, I'd seen too many arguments that ended in slammed doors and hurt feelings, so I became a professional conflict avoider. I'd rather swallow my frustration than risk a fight.

It took me years to learn that avoiding conflict doesn't make it disappear, it just makes it go underground where it festers and grows.

My friend Sarah learned this lesson when her twenty-year marriage nearly ended over what seemed like constant bickering. They were fighting about everything - money, kids, household responsibilities, where to spend holidays. She was ready to throw in the towel because she thought all that conflict meant they were incompatible.

Then their marriage counselor asked them to look deeper. What were they really fighting about? It turned out that underneath all those surface disagreements was one core issue: they both felt unappreciated and taken for granted. Once they recognized that pattern, they could address the real problem instead of just battling symptoms.

I've learned that conflict isn't the problem - it's often the solution trying to emerge. Those uncomfortable moments when you're not seeing eye to eye? That's your relationship trying to grow, trying to find a new level of understanding.

Getting to the Heart of It

The most important question I've learned to ask during any disagreement is: "What is this really about?"

Because it's rarely about what you think it's about.

I remember a heated discussion I had with my daughter when she was in college about her spending habits. I was frustrated that she was going over budget, and she was defensive about my "micromanaging." We went round and round about receipts and allowances until I finally stopped and asked myself what was really bothering me.

It wasn't the money, it was that I was scared she wasn't developing responsible habits that would serve her as an adult. And her resistance wasn't really about wanting to spend freely, it was about feeling like I didn't trust her judgment.

Once we talked about those deeper concerns, the surface issue became much easier to resolve.

The technique I use now is what I call the "three why's." When something bothers me, I ask myself why three times:

- Why does this bother me?
- Why does that matter to me?
- Why is that important?

Usually by the third "why," I've gotten to the real issue.

Fighting Fair

Over the years, I've learned that how you fight matters more than whether you fight. Some conflicts bring you closer together; others drive wedges between you. The difference is in the approach.

One game-changer for me was learning to use "I" statements instead of "you" accusations. Instead of "You never listen to me" (which immediately puts someone on the defensive), I learned to say "I feel unheard when we're discussing this."

It sounds like a minor change, but it shifts everything. The first version is an attack; the second is information about your experience.

My sister mastered this technique with her teenage son. Instead of saying "You're being disrespectful," she started saying "I feel dismissed when you walk away while I'm talking." Amazing how much more willing he became to engage when he didn't feel like he was being accused of being a bad person.

Another crucial skill is learning when to pause. When emotions are running high, we're not our smartest selves. I've learned to recognize when I'm getting flooded with feelings and to call a timeout, as mentioned in the last chapter.

"I need a few minutes to calm down so I can think clearly about this" has become one of my most useful phrases. It's not avoiding the conversation - it's ensuring the conversation will be productive when we have it.

The Art of Compromise

Real compromise isn't about both people giving up what they want. It's about finding creative solutions that honor what matters most to each person.

My husband and I learned this when we were planning our first big vacation together. I wanted relaxation - beaches, spa days, sleeping in. He wanted adventure - hiking, museums, exploring new cities. Our first instinct was to take turns: beach for three days, then adventure for three days.

But that meant each of us would spend half our vacation doing something we didn't really want to do.

Instead, we got creative. We found a coastal city with great hiking trails, amazing food scenes to explore, and a hotel with a spa. I could have my relaxing mornings and he could have his adventurous afternoons. We both got what we needed because we looked beyond our initial positions to understand our underlying desires.

The key is distinguishing between your needs and your wants. Needs are non-negotiable - things like feeling respected, feeling safe, feeling valued. Wants are preferences that might have some flexibility.

In our vacation example, my need was for genuine rest and restoration. My want was specifically for beach time. His need was for stimulation and discovery. His want was specifically for mountain hiking. Once we understood our real needs, we could find multiple ways to meet them.

When Things Get Stuck

Sometimes, despite your best efforts, you hit an impasse. You both understand each other's position, you've looked for creative solutions, but you still can't find a path forward.

This is when stepping into each other's shoes becomes invaluable. I learned this technique from watching my parents work through a major disagreement about my father's retirement plans. They were completely stuck until my mother said, "Let me try to argue your side for a minute."

She spent ten minutes genuinely trying to advocate for his position, and something shifted. Not because she changed her mind, but because he felt truly understood for the first time in their discussion. That understanding created space for a solution they hadn't seen before.

Sometimes you need outside perspective. This doesn't necessarily mean professional counseling - though that can be incredibly helpful. It might mean talking to a trusted friend who knows you both well, or even just explaining the situation to someone neutral and seeing what questions they ask.

My neighbor became an unofficial mediator for me and my husband during our great "Christmas traditions" debate. Just having to explain our positions to someone else helped us see where we were being rigid and where there was room for creativity.

Building Your Conflict Resolution Toolkit

The best time to develop your conflict resolution skills is when you're not in conflict. Think of it like emergency preparedness - you don't want to be figuring out your evacuation plan when the house is on fire.

Sit down with your partner when things are calm and talk about how you want to handle disagreements. What are your ground rules? Maybe it's no interrupting, no name-calling, no bringing up past grievances. Maybe it's agreeing to take breaks when emotions get too high, or establishing a signal that means "I'm feeling overwhelmed right now."

My husband and I have what we call our "conflict resolution charter." It includes things like:

- Either person can call a timeout, no questions asked
- We focus on the current issue, not past complaints
- We assume positive intent unless proven otherwise
- We're working toward a solution, not toward being right

Having these agreements in place makes it much easier to navigate conflicts when they arise.

The Growth Mindset

Perhaps the most important shift I've made is seeing conflict as information rather than threat. When my husband and I disagree about something, instead of thinking "Oh no, we have a problem," I try to think "Interesting, we're seeing this differently. What can we learn from that?"

This mindset has transformed not just my romantic relationships, but my relationships with my children, my friends, and even difficult coworkers. Conflict becomes curiosity instead of combat.

It's not always easy, and I don't always get it right. But I've learned that the relationships that grow stronger over time are the ones where both people are willing to work through their differences instead of avoiding them or letting them fester.

Every resolved conflict is like a deposit in your relationship's trust account. You learn that you can weather storms together, that you can disagree and still love each other, that you can work as a team even when you don't see eye to eye.

And that foundation of trust makes everything else - the joy, the intimacy, the everyday partnership - stronger and more resilient.

To complement this chapter, the following resources are available to download at the end of the book.

- "I feel' cheat sheet.

Non-Verbal Communication

I was having coffee with my friend Janet last week when I noticed something interesting. She was telling me about how well things were going with her new relationship, but her shoulders were hunched, her arms were crossed, and she kept fidgeting with her napkin. Her words said "everything is great," but her body was telling a completely different story.

When I gently asked if she was really as happy as she sounded, she paused, then admitted she was actually feeling anxious about how quickly things were moving. Her body had been broadcasting her true feelings the whole time.

That's the thing about non-verbal communication - we're all doing it constantly, whether or not we realize it. And often, our bodies are much more honest than our words.

The Language Your Body Speaks

I learned about the power of body language the hard way during a job interview years ago. I thought I was presenting myself as confident and capable, but I betrayed my words through unintended actions. I was sitting back in my chair (which probably looked disengaged), avoiding eye contact (which might have seemed evasive), and fidgeting with my pen (which likely appeared nervous).

Despite having all the right qualifications and giving what I thought were good answers, I didn't get the job. The feedback? They weren't sure I was really interested in the position.

That experience taught me that people are constantly reading signals I didn't even know I was sending.

Eye contact has become one of my most valuable communication tools. When my daughter talks to me about something important, I've learned to put down whatever I'm doing and look at her. The difference is remarkable, she opens up more, shares deeper concerns, and seems to feel truly heard in a way that doesn't happen when I'm half-listening while doing dishes.

But eye contact isn't universal. I learned this when my husband's family visited from another culture where direct eye contact, especially from younger to older family members, is disrespectful. What I interpreted as rudeness or disinterest was actually their way of showing respect. It was a good reminder that non-verbal cues don't mean the same thing to everyone.

Posture tells a story too. I notice that when I'm feeling defensive or overwhelmed, my shoulders creep up toward my ears and my arms naturally cross. When I catch myself doing this during a conversation, it's usually a sign that I need to pause and check in with what I'm really feeling.

Reading Between the Lines

One of the most valuable skills I've developed is learning to notice when someone's words and body language don't match. This has been especially important in my relationships with family members who weren't always direct about their feelings.

My mother, for example, would often say she was "fine" when clearly she wasn't. But I learned to read the signs, the tight smile, the way she held her shoulders, the slightly sharper tone. Once I started responding to what her body was telling me instead of just her words, our relationship improved dramatically.

"You seem stressed, Mom. What's really going on?" became much more effective than accepting her surface-level "I'm fine."

I see this pattern in couples all the time. One partner says they're not upset, but they're sitting with their back turned, speaking in clipped sentences, avoiding touch. The other partner gets confused because they're responding to the words ("I'm not upset") while ignoring the much louder non-verbal message.

Learning to trust what you observe, not just what you hear, has been relationship-changing for me.

Barbara & Arlan's Story:

> Barbara (83) and Arlan (84) have been married for 61 years. Living in the USA, their communication style is as seasoned as their relationship, straightforward, and built on decades of shared experience.

> While they skipped the first few questions of the survey, what they answered reveals a quiet confidence. Both say they feel safe being emotionally honest and vulnerable with each other. They talk about emotional needs occasionally, and haven't had to rebuild trust in their relationship. When asked about the last time they felt connected, their answer was simple and

powerful: "For us, continuously, we are very open with each other."

They describe their style of communication as "direct and to the point," though they also say their communication styles are "totally different." That difference seems to play out with humor and patience. When asked about recurring challenges, they wrote: "The husband usually says no to the wife's suggestions,,but she remains quiet during the debate, and he actually comes around to her point of view." It's a moment of levity that hints at their unspoken teamwork.

They haven't discussed love languages, but they know them: "I know mine, and we actually know each other's." After 61 years, it shows.

What works well for them is being direct. No games, no guesswork, just honesty, and consistency. And while they haven't had a big turning point in how they communicate, perhaps that's because they've been showing up the same way for each other all along.

Their advice to other couples is straightforward and full of truth: "Be open and direct in your approach and see that compromise is important."

My thoughts:

Barbara and Arlan's responses reflect the wisdom and rhythm that only six decades of partnership can bring. Their answers are direct and filled with understated affection. There's humor, honesty, and a deep sense of trust that's clearly been built over time. While their styles may differ, their approach is united: openness, directness, and patience. You get the sense that they don't just communicate well, they understand each other in a way that comes from years of listening, adjusting, and growing side by side.

Reflection Prompt:

What does "being direct" mean in your relationship? Are there moments where holding back complicates things more than it helps, and how can you create more space for honesty?

When Your Body Betrays Your Words

I was telling my husband about an exciting opportunity at work last year, but as I spoke, I realized I was unconsciously shaking my head. My words were saying "this is great," but my body was saying "I have serious doubts about this."

He noticed the disconnect and asked, "Are you actually excited about this, or are you trying to convince yourself you should be?"

That question stopped me in my tracks. I thought I was eager, but my body revealed that I had reservations I hadn't even acknowledged to myself.

This kind of misalignment between words and body language happens more often than we realize. We say we're happy while slumping our shoulders. While: Scrolling on our phones, we claim to be listening. We insist we're not angry while speaking through gritted teeth.

The problem is that people almost always believe the body language over the words. And they should, our bodies are much harder to control and often betray what we're feeling.

I've learned to do regular "body checks" during important conversations. Am I matching my posture to my message? If I'm trying to convey openness, are my arms uncrossed? If I want to show engagement, am I making appropriate eye contact?

This isn't about manipulation or putting on a performance. It's about making sure all parts of me are communicating the same message, so there's no confusion about what I intend.

The Art of Presence

One of the best gifts you can give someone is your full physical presence. Not just being in the same room, but actually being there, body language open, attention focused, energy directed toward them.

I learned this from watching my grandmother with us grandchildren. When we talked to her, she would turn her entire body toward us, lean in slightly, and give us her complete attention. Even as a child, I could feel how special that made me feel.

Now I try to do the same thing. When my husband wants to tell me about his day, I close the laptop, turn away from whatever I'm doing, and face him. It's a small physical shift that makes a huge difference in the quality of our conversation.

My daughter mentioned recently that she can always tell when I'm really listening versus when I'm just being polite. "When you're really listening, Mom, your whole body is listening, not just your ears."

That observation has stuck with me because it captures something important: genuine attention is a full-body experience.

Reading the Room

Years of observing relationships, my own and others, has taught me to pay attention to the subtle signals people send. The way someone's energy changes when a certain topic comes up. How their posture shifts when they feel defensive. The difference between a genuine smile and a polite one.

My sister has mastered this skill with her teenage daughter. She can tell from the way her daughter walks in the door whether she's had a good day or a rough one, whether she wants to talk or needs space, whether something big is on her mind.

"I don't read her mind," my sister told me. "I just pay attention to what her body is telling me."

This kind of awareness has made her a much more effective parent because she can respond to her daughter's actual emotional state rather than just the words she says.

Making It All Work Together

The goal isn't to become a body language expert who analyzes every gesture. It's to become more aware of the constant non-verbal conversation happening in your relationships.

Sometimes this means noticing when your own body language doesn't match your intentions. Other times it means picking up on signals that your partner is struggling, even when they have said nothing.

My husband and I have developed what we call "check-ins" when we notice a disconnect. "I'm hearing you say you're fine, but you seem tense. What's really going on?" or "I want to make sure I'm understanding you. Can you help me see what you're feeling right now?"

These conversations have prevented countless misunderstandings and helped us address issues before they become problems.

The beautiful thing about non-verbal communication is that once you pay attention to it, your relationships become richer and more authentic. You're not just exchanging words, you're truly seeing and being seen by the people you care about.

And that kind of connection, where all of you is communicating with all of them, is where real intimacy begins.

Building and Rebuilding Trust

Trust broke in my first marriage on a Tuesday afternoon in March. Not in some dramatic, movie-scene way, but quietly, over something that seemed almost trivial at the time. My ex-husband had promised to handle an important financial matter, and when I discovered weeks later that he'd forgotten, again, something inside me just... deflated.

Money and the task were not the problem. It was the pattern. The promises made and broken, the responsibilities dropped, the feeling that I couldn't count on him for the things that mattered. Trust, I learned, rarely shatters in one big moment. It erodes, grain by grain, until one day you realize the foundation you thought you were standing on has worn away.

But I also learned something else: trust can be rebuilt. It's painstaking work, and it's not always successful, but it's possible. The relationship where I first lost trust couldn't be saved, but the lessons I learned about trust helped me build something stronger the second time around.

The Daily Architecture of Trust

Trust lives in the small moments. It's my husband remembering that I have an important meeting today and asking how it went. It's me keeping his confidences when he shares something vulnerable. It's both of us doing what we say we'll do, when we say we'll do it, even when it's inconvenient.

My friend Carol learned this after her husband's affair nearly ended their twenty-five-year marriage. The big betrayal was devastating, but rebuilding trust happened through tiny actions repeated over months and years. Him coming home when he said he would. Her sharing her feelings instead of withdrawing. Him being transparent about his whereabouts. Her choosing to believe his explanations instead of assuming the worst.

"It was like building a house with tweezers," she told me. "Every day, we had to choose to do the work of trusting each other again. Some days we did better than others."

Trust in daily life looks like reliability in the mundane things. When my husband says he'll pick up milk on the way home and actually does it, that's a tiny deposit in our trust account. When I promise to be ready to leave at seven and I'm ready at seven, that's another deposit.

It sounds silly until you realize how many slight disappointments can add up. How many "I forgot" or "I thought you said..." or "Something came up" it takes before someone wonders if they can count on you.

When Trust Gets Damaged

Sometimes trust breaks in obvious ways, lies, betrayals, major promises broken. But more often, it's death by a thousand small cuts. The friend who always shows up late. A partner who makes promises but doesn't keep them. The family member who shares your private business despite asking them not to.

My daughter went through this with a close friend in college. No big dramatic fight, just a gradual realization that this person didn't keep confidences, didn't follow through on plans, and somehow always had an excuse for why things weren't her fault. The friendship didn't end in anger, it just... faded, because my daughter stopped investing in someone she couldn't rely on.

In romantic relationships, trust damage often starts with small things and grows. You stop sharing certain worries because your partner dismisses them. You stop making plans together because they often change them last minute. Because: Since your feelings might be used against you, you stop being vulnerable.

The tricky thing about trust is that once it erodes, it affects everything. You question motives, reading negative intentions into innocent actions, holding back parts of yourself to avoid potential disappointment.

The Hard Work of Rebuilding

Rebuilding trust requires something that doesn't come naturally to most of us: radical honesty and consistent follow-through over an extended period.

When my current husband and I first got together, I was carrying trust issues from my previous relationship. I tested him in ways that weren't fair—setting little traps to see if he'd disappointed me like I'd been disappointed before.

He called me on it. "I can see you're waiting for me to let you down," he said one day. "But I'm not him, and this isn't that relationship. What do you need from me to feel secure?"

That conversation changed everything because it made the invisible visible. Instead of me testing and him failing tests he didn't know he was taking, we could talk openly about what trust looked like for both of us.

What I now see as "trust protocols", specific, concrete ways we'd support one another, were established by us. We'd be where we said we'd be when we said we'd be there. Sharing our genuine feelings, rather than saying "fine" when we weren't, is what we'd do. We'd keep each other's confidences sacred. We'd own our mistakes instead of making excuses.

The formality masked its liberating nature. Having clear expectations removed the guesswork and gave us both a roadmap for building something solid.

Creating Emotional Safety

Trust isn't just about reliability, it's about emotional safety. Sharing your fears without judgment, is that possible? Can you admit mistakes without being attacked? Can you be imperfect without losing love?

I watch couples navigate this all the time. One partner shares a worry, and instead of comfort, they get advice or dismissal or criticism. They share excitement about something, and it gets minimized or ignored. They admit to a struggle, and then they're getting a lecture about what they should have done differently.

After a few experiences like that, people stop sharing. And when people stop sharing, intimacy dies.

My sister mastered the art of creating emotional safety with her husband during a difficult period when he was dealing with job loss and depression. Instead of trying to fix him or cheer him up or give him advice, she just... listened. His feelings were validated by her. She assured him that his worth wasn't tied to his employment status. She created a space where he could fall apart without judgment.

"I couldn't take away his pain," she told me, "but I could make sure he didn't have to carry it alone."

That's what emotional safety looks like, knowing that your person will sit with you in the difficult emotions instead of trying to rush you out of them.

Amelia & Ben's Story:

> Ben (26) and Amelia (28) from the UK have been together for five to six years and describe their communication as "a work in progress." That phrase captures the heart of their experience, two people who care deeply, even as they work through the challenges of understanding each other better.

> When asked if they feel heard, both answered "sometimes." They handle disagreements by arguing and then cooling off, and while they feel safe being honest, they talk about emotional needs only rarely.

> Their communication styles are the opposite. Amelia is open and expressive, while Ben avoids conflict. She finds texting easier; he bottles things up until he can't anymore. It's a dynamic many couples will recognize, different styles clashing, but with the right intention underneath.

> Despite the friction, there's closeness. They feel most connected when they have space to be present with each other,

like on holiday, with nothing else competing for their attention. They've had to rebuild trust, and what helped was being "upfront and honest." That experience shaped their turning point: a big fight that eventually led to clearer communication.

Their recurring challenge is fighting about money, but their advice to others reflects maturity and insight: "Listen. Be compassionate. Understand each other."

My Thoughts

Ben and Amelia's responses are honest, relatable, and reflective of a couple in the earlier stages of navigating long-term communication habits. There's rawness here, conflict, effort, and an obvious desire to do better. Their story will resonate with younger couples figuring it out in real time. It's a reminder that growth doesn't have to be perfect, it just has to be intentional.

Reflection Prompt:

What happens when your communication styles clash? Are there ways you can meet in the middle, especially during stress or conflict, to stay connected instead of reactive?

The Art of Deep Connection

Beyond trust lies intimacy, that sense of being truly known and accepted by another person. Not just the surface-level stuff, but the real you. The parts you're proud of and the parts you'd rather hide. The dreams you're afraid to say out loud and the fears that wake you up at night.

Emotional intimacy has been the biggest surprise of my second marriage. I thought I'd experienced it before, but I realize now that what I had was closeness, which is different. Closeness is sharing activities and daily life. Intimacy is sharing your inner world.

The difference became apparent to me when my husband and I went through a stressful period involving aging parents and job changes and health scares all at once. Instead of pulling apart under the pressure, we somehow grew closer. We started sharing not just what was happening, but how we were feeling about what was happening. Not just the facts, but the fears, the hopes, the vulnerable places.

I remember one night, completely overwhelmed, I admitted to him I was terrified I wasn't strong enough to handle everything on my plate. Instead of reassuring me I was strong (which would have missed the point), he said, "You don't have to be strong enough. We'll figure it out together."

That's when I understood the difference between being loved for your strengths and being loved including your weaknesses.

Simple Practices That Create Connection

Some of the most powerful intimacy-building practices are surprisingly simple. My husband and I started doing what we call "daily appreciations", at dinner, we each share one thing we appreciated about the other that day. It could be something big or something tiny. The act of actively noticing positive things about each other and saying them out loud has transformed how we see each other.

We also established "feeling check-ins"—not elaborate therapy sessions, just a few minutes each day where we ask, "How are you really doing?" and wait for honest answers. Sometimes the answer is "Great!" Sometimes it's "I'm worried about..." or "I'm excited about..." or "I'm feeling disconnected and I'm not sure why."

These aren't heavy conversations. They're just moments of genuine connection that keep us tuned into each other's emotional landscape.

My friend Susan and her husband created what they call "story time", one evening a week where they take turns sharing a story from their past that the other person hasn't heard before. After fifteen years of marriage, they discovered there were still chapters of each other's lives they didn't know about. These stories became windows into understanding why each of them reacts to certain situations the way they do.

The Courage to Be Seen

Real intimacy requires vulnerability, and vulnerability requires courage. It means showing up as your authentic self instead of the version you think your partner wants to see.

I spent years in my first marriage trying to be the "perfect wife", never demanding, always accommodating, constantly managing my own needs to avoid any possibility of conflict. I thought I was being loving, but what I was doing was hiding. How can someone love you if they don't know you?

Learning to be vulnerable has been one of the hardest and most rewarding aspects of personal growth for me. It started with small things, admitting when I was confused instead of pretending to understand, saying "I need help" instead of struggling alone, expressing disappointment instead of saying "it's fine" when it wasn't fine.

The amazing thing about vulnerability is that it's contagious. Partner Permission: Your authentic presence allows your partner to be authentic as well. When you admit your fears, they can admit theirs. When you share your dreams, they feel safe sharing theirs.

It's not about dumping all your emotional baggage on someone else. It's about letting down the walls that keep you separate and isolated, allowing someone to truly see and know you.

Building Intimacy Over Time

Intimacy isn't a destination you reach; it's a quality you cultivate. It deepens through shared experiences, honest conversations, and the gradual accumulation of trust and understanding.

Some of my deepest moments of connection with my husband have happened during ordinary activities, driving somewhere together, working in the garden, making dinner. When you create space for real conversation in everyday life, intimacy flourishes.

The goal isn't to share every thought or feeling, that would be overwhelming for both of you. It's to create an environment where authentic sharing feels safe and welcome, where you both know you can be yourselves without fear of judgment or rejection.

That kind of emotional safety becomes the foundation for everything else in your relationship. When you know you're truly accepted, flaws and all, you can relax into love in a way that transforms everything else about how you connect.

To complement this chapter, the following resources are available to download at the end of the book.

- **Trust building checklist.**

Communication Styles and Adaptation

My sister and I learned we had completely different communication styles during a family crisis when our father was in the hospital. I was firing off questions to the doctors, making lists, organizing shifts, basically taking charge of everything. Meanwhile, she was sitting quietly by his bedside, holding his hand, picking up on emotional cues I was completely missing.

By the end of the week, we were both frustrated with each other. I thought she wasn't engaged enough; she thought I was being too aggressive and overwhelming. It wasn't until we actually talked about it we realized we were both trying to help, we just had different ways of showing care.

That experience taught me something crucial: there's no "right" way to communicate. There are just different styles, and problems arise when we don't understand or appreciate each other's approach.

The Four Faces of Communication

Over the years, I've noticed that most people fall into one of four communication patterns, though we all probably use different ones depending on the situation.

Assertive communicators are the ones who can say what they mean directly but kindly. My friend Maria is like this, she can tell you she disagrees with you while making you feel respected. She maintains eye contact, speaks calmly, and somehow manages to be both honest and gentle. When she has a problem, she addresses it head-on, but without making you feel attacked.

Passive communicators are the peacekeepers. This was me for most of my first marriage, always deferring, rarely expressing my actual opinions, constantly trying to avoid any possibility of conflict. My husband would ask where I wanted to go for dinner, and I'd say "wherever you want" even when I had strong preferences. I thought I was being accommodating, but I was creating problems because my needs weren't being met, and he never got to know what I really wanted.

Aggressive communicators dominate conversations and push their point across, often with little concern for how others feel. I've watched couples where one partner uses volume and intensity to win arguments. It might work in the short term, but it usually shuts down actual communication because the other person stops sharing.

Passive-aggressive communicators are perhaps the trickiest to deal with. They express frustration indirectly, through sarcasm, silent treatment, or doing things like agreeing to help but then "forgetting" or doing a poor job. My ex-mother-in-law was a master at this. She'd say "fine" about dinner plans while sighing heavily and making it clear she wasn't actually fine at all.

Where Our Styles Come From

Our communication patterns usually start in childhood. I grew up in a house where expressing powerful emotions was "making a scene," so I learned to stuff down my feelings and try to keep everyone happy. My husband grew up in a family where people said exactly what they thought, sometimes loudly, but then hugged it out and moved on.

Neither approach is better, but when you put them together without understanding the differences, you get confusion. Early in our relationship, when he'd raise his voice during a discussion, I'd shut down, thinking we were having a terrible fight. Meanwhile, he was just expressing himself normally and couldn't understand why I was withdrawing.

I see cultural differences play out in communication all the time, too. My neighbor is from a culture where directness is rude, so she communicates through hints and context. Her American-born husband spent years missing her signals because he was waiting for her to just say what she wanted. Once they understood this difference, they could bridge it, she learned to be more direct with him, and he learned to pay attention to her subtler cues.

When Styles Clash

The problems happen when different communication styles collide and neither person understands what's happening. I watched this play out with my daughter and her college roommate. My daughter is direct and says what she means. Her roommate was more indirect and expected my daughter to pick up on hints and mood changes.

When the roommate was upset about something, she'd give subtle signals, being a little quieter, not making eye contact, expecting my daughter to notice and ask what was wrong. But my daughter would just think she was tired or busy. Meanwhile, when my daughter was upset, she'd speak plainly, which the roommate interpreted as aggressive or confrontational.

They both thought the other person didn't care about their feelings, when they simply had different ways of expressing and recognizing emotional needs.

Sometimes the problem goes deeper than just style differences. I've learned to watch for patterns that suggest something more concerning is happening. If someone turns every conversation back to themselves, avoids taking responsibility for anything, dismisses your feelings, or uses manipulation to control outcomes, those aren't just communication style differences, they're red flags.

I had a friend whose husband would do this thing where anytime she brought up a concern, he'd somehow turn it around, so she ended up apologizing to him. She'd start a conversation about feeling neglected, and by the end, she'd be comforting him about how hard his life was. It took her years to recognize this pattern and understand that healthy communication means both people's feelings and perspectives matter.

Learning to Bridge the Gap

The key to working with different communication styles is empathy, trying to understand why someone communicates the way they do instead of judging them for not communicating like you.

When I realized my husband's directness wasn't aggression but just his normal way of expressing himself, I could detach. When he understood that my need for processing time wasn't avoidance,way, but just how I work through things, he could give me space without feeling shut out.

We learned to adapt to each other's styles. If I need to discuss something important, I give him a heads up: "I want to talk about our budget this evening after dinner." That way, he's prepared for a focused conversation instead of being ambushed. When he has something urgent to discuss, he's learned to check in with me first: "Are you in a place to talk about something, or should we plan to do this later?"

David & Jann's Story:

David (70) and Jann (63) have been married for over a decade and live in the U.S. When asked to describe their communication, they both agree: "Pretty good, we have our moments."

That honesty runs through many of their answers. While Jann feels heard when she talks, David admits it's only "sometimes." In disagreements, their approaches differ too. Jann withdraws, while David says they usually argue and then cool off. Still, both say they feel emotionally safe being vulnerable with each other and regularly talk about their emotional needs, a strength that not all couples share.

Their communication styles reflect their personalities. David describes himself as "direct and to the point," while Jann leans toward avoiding conflict. Interestingly, David believes their styles are very similar, but Jann notes there's a bit of a difference, perhaps another sign of how each experiences their interactions a little differently.

One area they haven't yet explored is love languages—they both said they weren't familiar with the concept. But what works for them is clear: uninterrupted quiet time, especially outside. "Going out to mow the lawn or work the land, there's something therapeutic about it," David shared. For Jann, distractions are the biggest challenge. "Too many things crowd out the quiet time we need." David agrees, mentioning the number of committees and boards he's involved in as a source of disconnection.

When asked if they'd had a breakthrough moment in their communication, both said no, but David added, "We're searching for a breakthrough, and because we're searching, it will happen." That optimism, quiet, persistent, and shared, might be the strongest insight of all.

My Thoughts

There's something quietly thoughtful in the way David and Jann relate to each other. Their answers reflect a couple who values space, physically and emotionally, as part of how they stay connected. They may not have had a breakthrough yet, but their willingness to keep searching for one says a lot. Sometimes, it's not about having it all figured out, it's about creating the moments where understanding grows.

Reflection Prompt:

What does "quiet time" look like in your relationship? How do you each create space to reconnect, without distractions?

Finding Your Rhythm Together

The goal isn't to change your natural communication style, it's to understand it and learn when to adapt it for better connection. I've learned to recognize when my tendency toward passive communication isn't serving me or my relationship. If something is bothering me, I've practiced speaking up sooner rather than letting it build up into resentment.

My husband has learned to soften his directness when we're discussing emotional topics. He's a problem-solver who wants to jump straight to solutions, but he's learned that sometimes I need him to listen and understand before we fix anything.

We practice something I call "style checking." If a conversation isn't going well, one of us might say, "Can we restart this? I think our styles are clashing." Then we take a breath and try a different approach.

With my daughter, I've learned that when she's in conflict-avoidance mode, pushing for immediate resolution just makes her shut down more. So I've learned to say something like, "I can see this is hard to talk about. Should we take a break and come back to it later?" That gives her the space she needs without abandoning the conversation entirely.

The Art of Adaptation

Learning to work with different communication styles has made all my relationships better, not just romantic ones. With my sister, I've learned to appreciate her gentle approach instead of seeing it as indecisiveness. She's learned that my directness comes from caring, not from trying to control everything.

The most important thing I've learned is that there's no single "right" way to communicate. There are just different approaches that work better in different situations with different people. The magic happens when you can recognize what the other person needs and adjust your approach accordingly.

This doesn't mean losing yourself or always accommodating others. It means being flexible enough to meet people where they are while still honoring your own communication needs.

When my husband and I have our weekly check-ins now, we sometimes talk about how our communication went that week. Did we feel heard? Were there moments when our styles clashed? What worked well? It's become a way of fine-tuning our connection and staying aware of how we're affecting each other.

Building Bridges Instead of Walls

The most successful couples I know aren't the ones who communicate alike, they're the ones who've learned to appreciate and work with their differences. They see their different styles as complementary rather than conflicting.

My friends Carol and her husband are a perfect example. She's assertive and direct; he's more reflective and needs time to process. Instead of seeing this as a problem, they've learned to use it as a strength. When they need to make important decisions, she brings the clarity and momentum, and he brings the thoughtfulness and consideration of all angles.

They've created what they call "discussion protocols", ways of handling important conversations that honor both their styles. For big decisions, she presents the issue and her initial thoughts. Then he takes time to think about it before they reconvene. For day-to-day stuff, they've learned to be more immediate and spontaneous.

The key is recognizing that different doesn't mean wrong. It just means you need to create space for both approaches to coexist and complement each other.

Learning to work with communication style differences has been one of the most valuable relationship skills I've developed. It's made me a better partner, parent, friend, and colleague. Because undefined, most relationship problems aren't about incompatibility, they're about misunderstanding. And once you understand how someone communicates and why, connection becomes so much easier.

Self-Reflection & Personal Growth

I was complaining to my sister about a frustrating conversation I'd had with my husband when she stopped me mid-sentence and said, "Annabel, you do realize you just described the exact same fight you had with him last month, right? And the month before that?"

She was right. I'd been having the same argument over and over, getting frustrated each time, but never stopping to ask myself what role I might play in this pattern.

That conversation was a wake-up call. I realized I'd been so focused on what he was doing wrong that I'd never examined what I might contribute to our communication problems.

The Mirror of Self-Awareness

Looking at your own communication habits is uncomfortable work. It's much easier to focus on what your partner is doing wrong than to examine your own patterns. But I've learned that the only person's communication I can change is my own.

I started paying attention to how I showed up in conversations, and what I discovered wasn't always flattering. I noticed that when I felt criticized, I'd get defensive and start explaining why I was right instead of actually listening to what was being said. When I was stressed, my tone would become sharp and impatient, even when discussing something completely unrelated to what was stressing me.

I also realized I had a habit of assuming negative intentions. If my husband seemed distracted during a conversation, I'd think he didn't care about what I was saying, instead of considering that he might just be tired or worried about something else.

My friend Linda went through this same process after her daughter pointed out that Linda always interrupted people when they were talking. "I thought I was being engaged and enthusiastic," Linda told me. "I did not know I was actually preventing people from finishing their thoughts." Once she noticed the pattern, she could start changing it.

The tricky thing about our communication habits is that they feel normal to us. We've been doing them for so long that we don't even notice them anymore. It's like having an accent. You don't hear it yourself, but it's obvious to everyone else.

Discovering Your Triggers

One of the most valuable things I learned about myself was identifying my emotional triggers—those specific things that send me straight into reaction mode without passing through rational thought.

For me, one big trigger is feeling dismissed or ignored. If I'm trying to tell my husband something and he keeps looking at his phone, or if he responds with a distracted "mm-hmm," I can feel my whole body tense up. In the past, I'd either explode with frustration or withdraw and sulk, neither of which was helpful.

Another trigger is feeling like I'm being blamed for something that isn't my fault. Even a mild suggestion that I might have done something differently can send me into defense mode, listing all the reasons I was right and the other person was wrong.

These triggers usually have deep roots. My sensitivity to being dismissed likely stems from being the youngest in a family where my opinions weren't always valued. My defensiveness around blame might stem from growing up with a parent who was quick to point out mistakes.

I learned to track my triggers by paying attention to my physical reactions. When I felt my shoulders tense up or my jaw clench during a conversation, that was a sign that something had been triggered. Learning to pause and ask myself, "What just happened? What am I reacting to?" helped me understand my patterns better.

The Practice of Honest Self-Examination

A few years ago, I started doing what I call "conversation post-mortems", reviewing important discussions to understand what went well and what didn't. Not to beat myself up, but to learn.

After a tough conversation with my daughter about her career choices, I sat down and thought about how I'd shown up. Had I listened to understand, or had I listened to formulate my response? Had I made her feel supported, or had I made her feel judged? Was I responding to what she actually said, or what I was afraid she meant?

That conversation hadn't gone well, and when I examined my role, I could see why. I'd spent most of the time thinking about all the reasons her plan wouldn't work instead of trying to understand why it was important to her. I'd asked questions that sounded supportive but were actually designed to poke holes in her reasoning.

Recognizing this pattern helped me approach our next conversation differently. Instead of going into problem-solving mode, I started with a genuine curiosity about her perspective.

My sister has gotten into the habit of doing quick "communication check-ins" with herself at the end of each day. She asks herself questions like: "Did I speak kindly today?" "Was I present during conversations, or was I distracted?" "Did I express my needs clearly, or did I expect people to guess what I wanted?"

"It's not about being perfect," she told me. "It's about being aware. When I notice I'm falling into old patterns, I can course-correct."

The Power of Putting Pen to Paper

I've never been much of a journal keeper, but during a difficult period in my life, dealing with my father's illness while navigating job stress and relationship challenges, a friend suggested I try writing my thoughts each day.

At first, it felt forced and awkward. What was I supposed to write about? It evolved into a way of sorting through the chaos in my head. I'd write about conversations that had bothered me, relationships that felt stuck, decisions I was struggling to make.

What surprised me was how much clarity came from just getting my thoughts out of my head and onto paper. Things that felt overwhelming and complicated when they were swirling around in my mind became more manageable when I wrote them down.

I started noticing patterns in my behavior that I'd been blind to. I'd write about being frustrated with my husband, then realize as I wrote that I'd been taking out work stress on him. I'd complain about feeling misunderstood, then see that I hadn't actually explained what I needed very clearly.

My daughter discovered journaling during college when she was struggling with anxiety. "It's like having a conversation with myself," she told me. "I can say things on paper that I'm not ready to say out loud yet. And sometimes, just writing about a problem helps me see solutions I couldn't see when it was all jumbled up in my head."

She started writing about her communication challenges with friends and romantic partners, and it helped her recognize some of her own patterns. She realized she had a tendency to avoid tough conversations until they became crisis situations, then wonder why people seemed to be blindsided by her feelings.

Different Ways to Reflect

Not everyone processes through writing. My husband is more of a verbal processor. He needs to talk things through, out loud. But even he's found value in taking a few minutes each day to review how his conversations went.

Some of my friends use voice recordings on their phones, talking to themselves about their day and their interactions. Others prefer more creative approaches, drawing, making lists, even going for walks where they analyze their communication patterns.

The method doesn't matter as much as the intention: regularly taking time to examine how you're showing up in your relationships.

My neighbor started what she calls "gratitude communication journaling". Instead of focusing on what went wrong, she writes down moments when communication went well.

She says this practice has trained her to notice positive communication moments that she used to take for granted, which has improved her overall relationship satisfaction.

The Growth That Comes from Seeing Yourself Clearly

Self-reflection isn't always comfortable. I've had to face some unflattering truths about myself—my tendency to shut down when I feel overwhelmed, my habit of making assumptions about what people mean instead of asking for clarification, my pattern of saying "fine" when I'm clearly not fine.

But this awareness has been incredibly freeing. Once I understood my patterns, I could start making different choices. Instead of getting defensive when my husband offered feedback, I could pause and ask myself, "Is there something useful in what he's saying?"

I've watched this same transformation in other people who've committed to honest self-examination. My friend Carol, who realized she was interrupting people because she was afraid of losing her train of thought, learned to jot down quick notes so she could listen fully and then respond. My brother, who discovered he was dismissive when people shared problems because he immediately jumped to solutions, learned to ask, "Do you want advice, or do you just need me to listen?"

The goal isn't to become a perfect communicator—that's impossible. The goal is to notice your patterns so you can make conscious choices about how you want to show up in your relationships.

Building New Habits

Self-awareness is just the first step. The real growth happens when you practice new ways of communicating based on what you've learned about yourself.

I've learned to recognize my early warning signs of getting triggered, the tension in my shoulders, the urge to interrupt, the feeling of my mind racing ahead to plan my defense. When I notice these signs, I can pause and take a breath before responding.

I've also learned to be more direct about my communication needs. Instead of expecting my husband to guess when I need to talk something through, I've learned to say, "I'm processing something and could really use your perspective when you have a few minutes."

My daughter has learned to catch herself when she's avoiding a tough conversation and ask herself, "What am I afraid will happen if I bring this up? And is that fear realistic?" Often, she realizes her anxiety about the conversation is worse than the conversation itself would be.

This work of self-reflection and growth never really ends. Our communication needs and patterns evolve as we do. But the habit of honest self-examination, of regularly checking in with yourself about how you're showing up in your relationships, becomes a foundation for continuous improvement and deeper connection.

The beautiful thing is that when you communicate more consciously and authentically, it gives other people permission to do the same. Self-awareness becomes a gift not just to yourself, but to everyone you're in a relationship with.

Creating a Safe Space for Vulnerability

I'll never forget the first time I told my current husband about my deepest fear, that I wasn't lovable enough to keep someone around for the long haul. We'd been together about a year, and I was terrified that if I showed him the scared, insecure parts of myself, he'd realize he'd made a mistake.

I remember sitting on our couch, heart pounding, as I tried to find the words. "There's something I need to tell you," I started, then promptly lost my nerve and said, "Never mind, it's not important."

He put down what he was doing, turned to face me, and said, "If it's important enough that you brought it up, it's important to me. Take your time."

That simple response, the way he made space for whatever I needed to say without pushing or dismissing, taught me what emotional safety feels like. It's not the absence of fear; it's the presence of acceptance.

Building a Haven for Honesty

Creating emotional safety in a relationship is like tending a garden. It requires patience, consistency, and the right conditions for vulnerable things to grow. You can't force someone to open up, but you can create an environment where they feel safe enough to choose to.

I learned this the hard way in my earlier relationships. I used to think that being close meant sharing everything, and I'd get frustrated when someone wasn't as open as I wanted them to be. I'd push for deeper conversations before we'd built the trust necessary to support them.

With my daughter, I made the same mistake. When she was a teenager, I'd get concerned about something and want to have a deep heart-to-heart. But teenage vulnerability doesn't work on adult timelines. The more I pushed for emotional intimacy, the more she'd retreat.

I finally learned to create the conditions for openness instead of demanding it. I started paying attention to when she wanted to talk, often late at night when she was supposed to be sleeping, or during car rides when we weren't making eye contact. I learned to follow her lead instead of forcing my agenda.

The breakthrough came one evening when she was upset about something at school. Instead of asking what was wrong or offering advice, I just sat with her. After about ten minutes of silence, she started talking. Not because I'd created the perfect therapeutic moment, but because I'd made space for whatever she needed to share.

The Trust That Enables Truth

Emotional safety is built through countless small interactions where someone shares something vulnerable and it's received with care. It's about proving, over and over, that you can be trusted with someone's tender places.

I've learned that when someone shares something vulnerable with me, my first impulse is often to reassure them or offer solutions. But I've discovered that usually what people need first is just to feel heard and understood.

This became clear to me when I was going through my divorce and needed people who could just sit with my confusion and pain without trying to fix it or rush me through it. The people who helped most weren't the ones who gave advice - they were the ones who could simply say, "That sounds incredibly difficult" and mean it.

Now when someone shares something painful with me, I try to resist the urge to make it better and instead focus on making them feel heard.

Walter & Robin's Story:

Walter (71) and Robin (73), married for years and living in the U.S., describe their communication as "pretty good—we have our moments." Like many long-term couples, they've developed a rhythm, even if it's not always smooth.

When asked whether they feel heard, both answered "sometimes." Disagreements tend to play out through arguments that eventually cool off, and while they do feel emotionally safe with each other, deeper emotional conversations happen only occasionally.

They've talked about love languages in the past but haven't applied them. Their communication styles differ a bit—one shared they tend to avoid conflict, which may explain why things can build up before being addressed. Still, there's care beneath the quiet. They feel closest during family gatherings, shared vacations, and small moments of connection that bring them back to the center.

One thing they know works? Waiting until the noise dies down. "Wait until it's quiet and it's not working," was how they put it, a slightly ambiguous but telling statement. It suggests that timing and space matter, especially for couples who aren't expressive or emotionally talkative.

They noted retirement finances as a recurring challenge and admitted they're still figuring some things out. Their biggest shift in communication hasn't come from big sit-downs, but from staying in touch during their workdays, often by phone.

Their advice to other couples? "Appreciate how important connection is and quality time."

My thoughts:

Walter and Robin's responses show a steady, lived-in partnership that doesn't need loud declarations to prove its strength. Their communication might not be perfect, and they admit that sometimes one of them 'tends to win' the argument, but there's a confidence in how they connect. Feeling close "every day, all day" is no small thing. It speaks to a relationship where presence means more than perfection, and where the foundation is strong, even if the volume stays low.

Reflection Prompt:

How do you and your partner stay connected when life feels routine or quiet? Are there simple rituals,, like a phone call, a shared task, or a quiet moment, that help you feel close with no need a big conversation?

The Fear That Keeps Us Silent

The biggest barrier to vulnerability isn't lack of things to share—it's fear of how those things will be received. We're all carrying stories, worries, and dreams that feel too precious or too scary to expose to potential judgment.

I spent years in my first marriage holding back parts of myself that I thought might be "too much." My tendency toward anxiety, my need for reassurance, my big dreams that might seem unrealistic. I convinced myself I was protecting the relationship, but I was actually preventing true intimacy from developing.

The irony is that by trying to be perfect and low-maintenance, I created distance. My ex-husband often said he felt like he didn't really know me, and he was right. How could he know me when I was constantly editing myself?

My sister went through something similar in her first serious relationship. She was so afraid of being seen as needy that she never asked for what she actually needed. When she was feeling insecure, she'd act like everything was fine. When she wanted more quality time together, she'd pretend to be perfectly content with the status quo.

The relationship eventually ended, and while there were many factors, one big one was that neither person felt truly known by the other. They'd been so careful to avoid vulnerability that they'd avoided real connection too.

Learning to Share Your True Self

Vulnerability doesn't mean dumping all your emotional baggage on someone without consideration for their capacity to hold it. It means gradually letting someone see the real you—including the parts that aren't polished or perfect.

I learned to start small. Instead of sharing my deepest fears right away, I'd share smaller truths. "I'm feeling a little anxious about this work presentation" instead of pretending everything was fine. "I was hurt when you canceled our plans" instead of saying "no problem" when it actually was a problem.

Each positive response to these smaller vulnerabilities built my confidence to share bigger things. When my husband responded to my work anxiety with empathy instead of trying to solve it, I felt safer sharing other worries. When he thanked me for being honest about feeling hurt instead of getting defensive, I learned that conflict could bring us closer together.

My daughter has become a master at this gradual approach to vulnerability. She'll begin conversations with a question such as, "Can I tell you something? Promise not to immediately offer advice."

It was funny because when she was younger she always said, Can I tell you something? And you don't get mad. My head would think, what now?

These little prefaces help her feel safer sharing because she's setting the terms for how she wants the conversation to go.

Creating the Right Conditions

The environment for vulnerable conversations matters. I've learned that trying to have a heart-to-heart while doing dishes or watching TV rarely works well. Vulnerability requires presence and attention.

My husband and I have found that some of our deepest conversations happen during walks together. There's something about being side by side instead of face to face that makes difficult topics feel less intense. The rhythm of walking seems to help us both process what we're sharing and hearing.

Other couples I know have found their own rituals for creating safe spaces. Some have weekly "feelings check-ins" where they make time to share their feelings. Others find car trips create natural opportunities for deeper conversations.

The key is being intentional about creating space for these conversations rather than hoping they will appear amidst busy life.

When Someone Trusts You with Their Truth

Learning how to receive someone's vulnerability with grace is just as important as learning how to share your own. When someone opens up to you, they're offering you a gift, the gift of seeing their authentic self.

I've learned that my first response in these moments sets the tone for everything that follows. If I jump into fix-it mode or try to reassure them that their feelings aren't valid, I'm telling them that their emotional experience is incorrect.

Instead, I try to start with simple acknowledgment: "That sounds really difficult," or "I can see why you'd feel that way." These responses validate their experience without trying to change it.

My sister taught me something valuable about this when she was going through her divorce. She said the friends who helped her most weren't the ones who tried to cheer her up or convince her she was better off without her ex. They were the ones who could sit with her in the sadness and fear without trying to rush her out of it.

"I needed people who could handle my pain without making it about their discomfort with seeing me hurt," she told me. That insight has shaped how I try to show up for people I care about when they're vulnerable with me.

The Courage to Be Seen

True intimacy requires the courage to let someone see you without your armor on. It means sharing not just your successes and strengths, but also your struggles and uncertainties.

I remember one conversation with my husband early in our relationship where I admitted that I sometimes felt jealous of his close relationship with his ex-wife (they co-parent successfully). I was terrified he'd think I was being irrational or controlling.

Instead, he thanked me for being honest and asked thoughtful questions about what triggered those feelings. We ended up having a conversation that helped us both understand each other better and establish some boundaries that made me feel more secure.

That experience taught me that vulnerability often leads to solutions and deeper connection rather than the rejection I'd feared.

Building Intimacy Over Time

The deepest emotional intimacy develops gradually, through countless moments of choosing openness over self-protection. It's built by proving to each other, again and again, that you can be trusted with tender things.

Some of my most meaningful conversations with my daughter have happened during ordinary moments, driving her to appointments, making dinner together, sitting on her bed before she goes to sleep. Vulnerability often emerges when we're not trying to force it.

The goal isn't to share every thought and feeling, that would be overwhelming for everyone involved. It's to create a relationship where authentic sharing feels safe and welcome, where both people know they can be themselves without fear of judgment or rejection.

That kind of emotional safety becomes the foundation for everything else in the relationship. When you know you're accepted, warts and all, you can relax into love in a way that transforms how you connect with each other.

Practical Exercises and Scenarios

Last month, my husband and I sat down to plan our budget for the year. What should have been a straightforward conversation about numbers turned into something much more complicated. I was excited about finally saving for the trip to Italy we'd been talking about for years. He was worried about whether we had enough set aside for home repairs and unexpected expenses.

Within ten minutes, we weren't talking about money anymore. We were talking about security versus dreams, practical versus optimistic, his need to feel prepared versus my need to feel like we were building toward something exciting.

Sound familiar? Money conversations have a way of revealing deeper differences that have nothing to do with actual dollars and cents.

When Money Talks Get Messy

Financial discussions can bring out our deepest fears and fundamental differences. I've watched couples argue about a grocery budget when they're really arguing about control. I've seen fights about vacation spending that are actually about different values around work and leisure.

My sister and her husband went through this when they were newlyweds. Every discussion about money turned into a battle, with her feeling like he was trying to control her spending and him feeling like she didn't understand their financial reality. They were both right, and they were both missing the point.

The breakthrough came when they stopped talking about specific purchases and started talking about what money meant to each of them. For her, spending represented freedom and the ability to be generous with people she loved. For him, saving represented security and protection against the financial instability he'd experienced growing up.

Once they understood the deeper motivations, they could honor both needs. They built generosity into their budget and created a security fund that made him feel safe. The fights about money decreased because they were finally addressing the actual issues underneath.

When my husband and I hit our budget impasse, I remembered my sister's experience. Instead of continuing to debate Italy versus home repairs, I asked him, "What would happen if we didn't have that emergency fund? What are you most worried about?"

His answer revealed that his concern wasn't really about the money, it was about feeling responsible for our financial security and not wanting to let me down if something unexpected happened. Once I understood that, I could appreciate his perspective and work with him to find a solution that addressed both our needs.

The Invisible Workload That Creates Conflict

Remember, in Chapter 1 when we talked about emotional labor, all the mental and emotional work that keeps households running smoothly? This shows up constantly in practical scenarios, often disguised as arguments about chores or responsibilities.

I see this play out with my friends all the time. One partner feels overwhelmed by managing the household's mental load, remembering appointments, planning meals, coordinating schedules, keeping track of what needs to be done. The other partner might be completely willing to help but doesn't see all the thinking and planning that goes into daily life.

My friend Carol finally exploded at her husband one Saturday morning because he asked her what was for dinner. "I don't know," she said. "Why is that always my job to figure out?" He was genuinely confused, he'd asked a simple question and offered to cook whatever she wanted.

But Carol's frustration wasn't about that one question. It was about being the default person responsible for meal planning, grocery shopping, keeping track of what food they had, knowing everyone's dietary preferences and schedule constraints. The question felt like one more thing on her endless mental to-do list. I'm sure this resonates with many of you. It does me.

Once they understood the real issue, they could address it. He took over meal planning for two days a week, which meant not just cooking but thinking ahead about what to make, checking what ingredients they had, and doing the shopping. She realized how much mental energy went into those decisions only when she didn't have to make them.

When Life Schedules Collide

Double-booking ourselves is so common in our busy lives, but how we handle these conflicts says a lot about our relationship priorities and communication patterns.

I remember an evening when my husband and I realized we'd both made plans, I'd committed to dinner with a friend who was going through a divorce, and he'd scheduled an important business dinner with potential clients. Both were important, neither could be rescheduled, and we only had one car that day.

My first instinct was to get annoyed at him for not checking with me first. His first instinct was to assume I should reschedule since his was work-related. We were both operating from the assumption that our priority was more important.

Then I remembered something we'd learned in our earlier communication work: start with the assumption that we're both trying to do the right thing, and focus on solving the problem together instead of figuring out who was in the wrong.

"Okay," I said, "we both have important commitments tonight. How can we make this work?" That simple reframe changed everything. Instead of arguing about whose plan was more valid, we became teammates solving a logistics problem. We figured out transportation alternatives and ended up both keeping our commitments.

That experience taught me that most scheduling conflicts aren't really about the schedule, they're about feeling heard and respected in the relationship.

Building Connection Through Small Daily Habits

Some of the most powerful relationship tools are simple. I started giving my husband one genuine compliment each day after reading about the impact of positive reinforcement on relationships. Not forced flattery, but actually noticing something I appreciated about him that day and mentioning it.

"I noticed how patient you were with the customer service rep this morning when our internet was down." "Thank you for thinking to grab me coffee when you went to the kitchen." "I love how you always make sure I'm comfortable with the temperature before adjusting the thermostat."

These tiny acknowledgments have had a huge impact on how we see each other. I've started noticing positive things more because I'm actively looking for them. He feels more appreciated, which makes him want to be even more thoughtful. It's created a positive cycle that took maybe thirty seconds a day to establish.

We also started doing what we call "micro check-ins"—five minutes each evening where we ask each other, "How are you really doing today?" Not "How was your day?" which usually gets a surface-level answer, but "How are you feeling about things?"

Sometimes the answer is "Great, actually," and we spend two minutes sharing something good that happened. Sometimes it's "I'm worried about my mom" or "I'm feeling overwhelmed at work," and we spend a few minutes really hearing each other.

These conversations rarely solve big problems, but they keep us connected to each other's emotional landscape so that when bigger issues arise, we're not starting from scratch.

The Rose, Thorn, and Bud Ritual

My daughter taught me this practice that she learned in college. At the end of the day, we each share a rose (something that went well), a thorn (something challenging), and a bud (something we're looking forward to).

It's become one of my favorite relationship practices because it creates space for the full range of human experience. You can celebrate stuff without toxic positivity, acknowledge the tough stuff without dwelling on it, and maintain hope by focusing on what's ahead.

Last week, my rose was a lovely conversation with an old friend. My thorn was feeling frustrated with a work project that wasn't coming together. My bud was looking forward to our weekend plans to visit the farmer's market.

This simple practice keeps us both invested in each other's daily experience and creates natural opportunities for support and connection.

Creating Space for Deeper Sharing

Once a week, my husband and I have what we call "real talk time", a longer conversation where we can share anything that's been on our minds. This isn't a formal therapy session, just dedicated time when we're both fully present and committed to really listening to each other.

These conversations have covered everything from work stress to family concerns to relationship dynamics to personal dreams and fears. Having a regular time for this kind of sharing means we don't let important things build up until they become urgent.

Sometimes we use prompts to get started: "What's been taking up mental space for you this week?" or "Is there anything you've been wanting to talk about but haven't found the right moment?" Other times, one of us just has something we've been thinking about.

The key is creating an environment where anything can be shared without judgment or immediate problem-solving. We listen first, ask questions to understand better, and then discuss what kind of support or response would be most helpful.

The Power of Mindful Moments

When conversations get heated or emotional, I've learned the value of taking a few deep breaths before responding. This sounds basic, but it's been revolutionary for our communication.

I used to react reflexively to anything that triggered me emotionally. If I felt criticized or misunderstood, words would come out of my mouth before my brain engaged. These quick reactions usually made things worse, not better.

Now I try to pause and take three slow breaths before responding to anything that brings up powerful emotions. Those few seconds give me space to consider what I want to say and how I want to say it.

My husband and I also started doing brief meditation together a few times a week, just five or ten minutes of sitting quietly and focusing on our breathing. It's not about becoming Zen masters; it's about practicing being present and calm together. This shared stillness has improved our ability to stay grounded during difficult conversations.

Your Toolkit for Real Life

At the end of this book, you'll find links to download practical tools that support everything we've talked about, conversation starters for when you're not sure how to begin a difficult discussion, reflection prompts to help you understand your own patterns, and quick reference guides for techniques like "I feel" statements.

These aren't complicated resources that require special training to use. They're simple tools designed to make it easier to put these ideas into practice in your everyday life.

The goal isn't to turn your relationship into a constant self-improvement project. It's to have easy access to techniques that can help when communication gets stuck or when you want to deepen your connection.

I keep some of these tools bookmarked on my phone for moments when I know we need to have an important conversation, but I'm not sure how to start it. Having concrete resources removes the guesswork and makes it easier to choose connection over avoidance.

Making It Sustainable

The practices that have lasted in my relationship are the ones that feel natural and helpful, not like homework assignments. Start with one or two things that appeal to you rather than trying to implement everything at once.

Maybe it's the daily compliment practice, or the weekly check-ins, or just remembering to pause and breathe before responding when emotions are high. Pick what resonates and try it for a few weeks before adding anything else.

The most important thing is consistency over perfection. A simple practice done regularly will have more impact than a complex system that you abandon after a few attempts.

These practical tools aren't magic solutions that will eliminate all relationship challenges. They're ways of staying connected and working through difficulties together rather than letting them drive you apart. And that ongoing choice to keep showing up for each other, conversation by conversation, is what builds the kind of relationship that can weather whatever life brings your way.

Apology and Forgiveness

You thought the conversation went fine, everything seemed normal. But later, your partner is upset, and you're left wondering what went wrong.

Misinterpretations like these are common in relationships, often stemming from assumptions and biases we may not even realize we're holding. These cognitive biases, such as the fundamental attribution error or negativity bias, can distort our perceptions, leading us to misjudge our partner's intentions. For example, you might assume your partner's abruptness is because of inherent impatience, rather than considering they might be stressed about work. Past relationships, too, cast long shadows over our current interactions. If you've been burned by betrayal before, you might question your partner's loyalty, even if they've given you no reason to doubt them. These patterns can create a minefield of misinterpretations, making clear communication even more essential.

When you're trying to express your feelings or intentions, clarity is key. When you're trying to express your feelings or intentions, clarity is key. One helpful approach is using "I" statements, a technique we explored in Chapter 4, along with the downloadable cheat sheet you'll find there. Another method is by using feedback loops. After you've shared something important, ask your partner to reflect on what they heard. This helps make sure your message landed the way you meant it. It keeps things clear, shows you're both listening, and helps build mutual respect and understanding.

Open dialogue is the lifeline of any thriving relationship. Keeping the conversation going, especially around your thoughts, feelings, and intentions, helps prevent misunderstandings before they take root. Regular check-ins don't have to be formal or forced. For us, it's sitting down with a coffee in the morning and chatting before the day starts. That time makes a difference.

Encourage questions and clarifications, too. If something doesn't sit right, ask about it. It's better to talk things through than to let small assumptions turn into big issues. When both people feel safe to ask, share, and clarify, communication becomes easier and more honest.

Exercise: Building Intentional Clarity

Role-playing exercises can be a fun and effective way to practice expressing intentions clearly. Choose a scenario with your partner where communication might break down—perhaps planning a holiday or discussing financial goals. Take turns playing each other's roles, focusing on using "I" statements and confirming understanding. This exercise helps you strengthen your communication skills while also giving you a better understanding of how your partner sees things. After a conversation, jot down your thoughts and feelings. Consider where you might have misunderstood or been misunderstood. This practice fosters greater self-awareness and highlights areas for improvement.

Communication in relationships is like a dance, requiring both partners to move in harmony. By recognizing and addressing the root causes of misinterpretation, you can create a space where both you and your partner feel understood and valued. It's not about eliminating conflict, but about navigating it with grace and empathy. As you practice these techniques, you'll likely find that your relationship becomes more resilient, equipped to handle the challenges that come your way.

Victoria & James's Story:

Victoria (55) and James (57) from the UK have been married for over a decade. When asked how they usually communicate, they both gave the same answer: "It's a work in progress." That theme carries through much of their story.

When it comes to feeling heard, both say it happens rarely. Their conflict styles also differ: James shared they talk it out, argue, then cool off, and sometimes one of them "wins" the disagreement. Victoria says they often withdraw or avoid the topic altogether. It's clear they don't always meet in the middle, but they're still showing up and trying.

Victoria said she's emotionally open depending on the situation, while James feels safe being vulnerable. He says they talk about emotional needs regularly, while she says only occasionally. These kinds of gaps are common in long-term relationships, especially when each partner communicates in different ways. Victoria keeps things to herself; James describes himself as open and expressive. Together, they agree their styles are "a bit different."

They've talked about love languages, but haven't put them into practice. And yet, they've found things that work: "resolving issues and agreeing to a way forward" has helped them navigate conflict. Their biggest challenge? "Inability to focus on each other's point of view." But even there, they've seen some growth. A difficult situation involving money became a turning point, one that led them to start being more open and honest with each other.

When asked when they last felt truly connected, they pointed to physical intimacy as a space where closeness still comes naturally. Their advice to other couples reflects their experience: "Just keep talking. Be nice to one another. And forgive the little things."

My thoughts:

This couple is living in the space between knowing they love each other and still learning how to communicate that. Their willingness to keep working on it, even when things feel mismatched, shows strength. Not every couple starts on the same page, but what matters is that they're still writing the story together.

Reflection Prompt:

What's one small way you and your partner could better focus on each other's point of view? Are there specific situations where listening feels harder, and how could you shift that dynamic?

Overcoming Emotional Disconnect

There's a certain heaviness that settles in when emotional disconnect creeps into a relationship. It can start with small things, like a lack of enthusiasm when sharing news or feeling like your partner is miles away even when they're sitting right next to you. Emotional withdrawal often manifests in subtle ways, such as reduced eye contact or rare, fleeting touches that once felt automatic. These signs can make you feel as if you're speaking into the void, where your words echo back without response. Physical absence, whether because of busy schedules or a preoccupation with personal devices, compounds this sensation of distance. When emotional and physical presence wane, it can make you feel you're living parallel lives, or coexisting rather than connecting. This disconnect doesn't always announce itself but sneaks in, creating a silent chasm that's tough to bridge without conscious effort.

Understanding the root causes of emotional disconnect is crucial for addressing it. Stress is a significant factor, often leaving partners too drained to engage. Whether it's the pressure of work deadlines or personal anxieties, stress can lead to emotional shutdown, where one or both partners retreat into themselves to cope. Unresolved conflicts also simmer beneath the surface, creating a tension that prevents genuine connection.

These lingering issues might be brushed aside in the moment, only to resurface at inopportune times, driving a wedge between you. Lifestyle changes, like relocating or shifting career trajectories, can also disrupt the emotional equilibrium. These transitions, while sometimes necessary, can unsettle the established patterns of interaction. Addressing these factors involves stress management techniques, like setting realistic goals and practicing relaxation exercises, to reduce tension and foster a supportive environment. Constructive conversations about unresolved issues can help clear the air, paving the way for renewed closeness.

Rebuilding emotional connection requires deliberate actions that foster warmth and intimacy. Creating shared experiences is a powerful way to rekindle emotional bonds. These experiences don't have to be extravagant, a simple weekend hike or a cooking class can work wonders in drawing you closer.

Shared memories act as the glue that binds you, reminding both of you of the joy and comfort that exists within the relationship. Engaging in mutual interests offers another avenue for connection. It could be as simple as watching a favorite series together or joining a local sports league.

These activities provide common ground, something to look forward to and enjoy as a team. Establishing rituals that promote togetherness can further reinforce this bond. Whether it's a nightly routine of unwinding together or a weekly date night, these rituals create a sense of stability and continuity, anchoring your relationship amidst life's chaos.

To deepen emotional intimacy, consider activities designed to enhance understanding and connection. Guided couple's meditation sessions can be particularly beneficial, offering a space for shared relaxation and mindfulness. This practice encourages you to be present with each other, fostering an awareness of the emotions and energies you bring into the relationship.

Sharing life goals and aspirations can also create a profound sense of unity. Discussing what you both envision for the future—whether it's career ambitions, family plans, or personal growth—aligns your paths and affirms your commitment to supporting each other's dreams. A simple yet effective practice is the "Highs and Lows" daily debrief. It involves sharing the best and most challenging moments of your day with each other, providing insight into your emotional landscape. This exercise not only enhances empathy but also keeps you attuned to each other's lives, reinforcing the emotional fabric of your relationship.

Strategies for Active Listening in Distracting Environments

Imagine trying to have a heartfelt conversation in a bustling cafe, where the clatter of cups and chatter of nearby patrons become an unwelcome soundtrack. Or perhaps you're at home, attempting to discuss something important while the TV blares in the background, and your phone vibrates with notifications. These distractions can quickly derail even the most earnest attempts at active listening. It's easy to get caught up in screens, checking a quick message turns into ten minutes of scrolling. But while we're glued to our phones, our partner can end up feeling ignored or pushed aside. Paying attention to how much time you spend online, especially when you're together, makes a real difference.

To combat these challenges, it's crucial to set boundaries for device usage during conversations. One approach is to establish tech-free zones or times, ensuring that when you're together, your focus remains on each other. (We do this) Creating a dedicated space for communication can also make a significant difference. This could be a cozy nook in your home where you both agree to sit and talk, free from the usual interruptions. By removing yourself from potential distractions, you signal to your partner that they have your undivided attention. This kind of intentional space can transform a routine conversation into a meaningful exchange, fostering a deeper connection.

Mindfulness can be a powerful ally in maintaining focus, helping you stay present even amid chaos. Before diving into a conversation, try engaging in mindful breathing techniques. Take a few deep breaths, inhaling through your nose and releasing through your mouth. This practice centers your mind and prepares you to deeply listen. Visual cues or reminders can also anchor your attention. Perhaps it's a small token you keep nearby, like a stone or a piece of jewelry, that reminds you to stay present. These little rituals reinforce the importance of being in the moment, encouraging you to absorb what your partner is saying without your mind wandering off.

To hone your active listening skills in real time, consider incorporating specific exercises into your routine. The "Listening without Interrupting" challenge is a simple yet effective way to practice. Take turns with your partner, allowing each of you to speak for a set amount of time without interruptions. Focus on truly hearing the other person, resisting the urge to jump in with your thoughts until they're done. Afterward, discuss how it felt to listen without interjecting, did you notice a difference in the conversation's depth or flow? This exercise can illuminate areas where you might need to improve and highlight the benefits of uninterrupted listening.

Partner feedback is another valuable tool for enhancing listening effectiveness. After a discussion, invite your partner to share their perspective on how well they felt listened to, and offer the same for them. This mutual exchange fosters a supportive environment where both of you can grow and refine your skills. Recording and reviewing conversations can also be enlightening. Listening back to these interactions allows you to identify moments where your focus might have waned or where you missed key points. This self-awareness is the first step toward becoming a more attentive listener.

Choosing to listen intently makes a tremendous difference. It shows your partner they matter. As you wrap up this chapter, think about one simple way you can put this into practice today. Minor changes in how we listen can lead to big shifts in how we connect. And that's exactly what the next chapter builds on.

Try This:

For the next 24 hours, be intentional about your listening. Put your phone away during conversations, make eye contact, and resist the urge to interrupt. Check in with yourself: Did your partner respond differently? Did you feel more connected?

To complement this chapter, the following resources are available to download at the end of the book.

- **Apology Language Quiz**
- **5 Apology Languages**

Empathy and Understanding

I was twenty-five when I learned the difference between sympathy and empathy, though it took me years to understand what that lesson meant for my relationships.

A close friend was going through the devastating loss of her mother, and I thought I was being supportive by constantly trying to cheer her up. I'd call with funny stories, invite her to movies, remind her of all the positive things in her life. I was baffled when she started seeming distant and eventually told me she needed some space.

Years later, when I was going through my own difficult time, she explained what had happened. "When I was grieving," she said, "your constant positivity made me feel like my sadness was wrong or too much for you to handle. I needed you to sit with me in the sadness, not try to pull me out of it."

That conversation taught me that sympathy says, "I feel bad for you, let me fix this." Empathy says, "I'm here with you in this tough place." It's a distinction that changed how I show up for people I care about.

Learning to Meet People Where They Are

Empathy is one of those skills I thought I had naturally until life taught me I really didn't. I was good at caring about people, good at wanting to help, but not always good at understanding what they were experiencing from their perspective.

The Barriers We Build

The biggest obstacle to empathy, I've discovered, is often our own emotional state. When I'm stressed or overwhelmed, my capacity for tuning into other people's feelings shrinks. I become preoccupied with my stuff and less able to really see what's happening with others.

I notice this especially in my marriage. When work is chaotic or I'm dealing with family stress, I can miss signals from my husband that would normally be obvious to me. He'll seem quieter than usual or more tired, and instead of checking in with him, I'll be too caught up in my own mental noise to notice.

Judgment is another barrier. I hate admitting this, but sometimes when someone is struggling with something I think they should be able to handle, I have trouble empathizing. My internal critic starts up: "Why don't they just..." or "If they would only..." That judgment creates distance between me and their experience. I still struggle with this, as I believe my son-in-law should 'man up' and sort out his shit.

The Art of Deep Listening

Real empathic listening differs from regular listening. It's not just hearing someone's words; it's trying to understand the emotions and experiences underneath those words.

I had to completely relearn how to listen during the difficult years of my first marriage. I was so focused on defending myself or preparing my counter-arguments that I wasn't actually hearing what my ex-husband was trying to tell me about his experience. Our conversations became battles instead of attempts to understand each other.

In my current marriage, I've tried to develop what I call "curiosity over judgment." When my husband shares something that bothers him, instead of thinking about whether his concern is valid or how I can fix it, I try to ask questions that help me understand his perspective.

"That sounds really frustrating," I might say. "What part of it bothers you most?" or "How long have you been carrying this worry?" These questions aren't designed to gather information so I can solve the problem, they're designed to help me understand his emotional experience.

This shift from problem-solving to understanding has transformed our conversations. He feels heard instead of managed, and I learn about his inner world instead of just hearing surface-level complaints.

When Empathy Changes Everything

I've seen empathy transform conflicts that seemed impossible to resolve. Not by making the problems disappear, but by creating understanding that allows people to work together instead of against each other.

This happened in my marriage during a period when we were constantly arguing about money. Every conversation about our budget turned into a battle, with me feeling like he was being impractical and him feeling like I was being controlling.

The breakthrough came when we each tried to explain the other person's perspective on money. I realized that his spending wasn't actually about being irresponsible, it was about his fear that we were so focused on saving for the future that we weren't enjoying our lives now. He understood that my desire to save wasn't about controlling him, it was about my deep fear of being financially vulnerable, something I'd experienced growing up.

Once we could see the fears and values driving each other's behavior, we could work together to find solutions that addressed both sets of concerns instead of just fighting about specific purchases.

Building Your Empathy Muscle

Empathy, I've learned, is a skill you can develop with practice. One exercise that's helped me is what I call "perspective-taking." When someone is telling me about a situation that's bothering them, I try to imagine not just how I would feel in their shoes, but how they specifically might be feeling given their personality, history, and current circumstances.

My daughter is naturally more sensitive than I am, so something that might feel like minor criticism to me could feel devastating to her. My husband processes stress internally while I process it out loud, so when he seems quiet and withdrawn, it might mean he's working through something important rather than being upset with me.

This kind of perspective-taking has helped me respond more appropriately to the people I love instead of assuming they experience things the same way I do.

I also practice what I call "empathy checking", asking people directly about their emotional experience instead of assuming I know. "It seems like you're feeling overwhelmed by this situation, is that accurate?" or "I'm hearing frustration in your voice. Is that what you're feeling, or am I missing something?"

These check-ins prevent me from making assumptions and give the other person a chance to clarify their experience.

The Ripple Effect

When you consistently show empathy to the people in your life, something beautiful happens: they start feeling safer being vulnerable with you. They share more of their real thoughts and feelings because they know you'll try to understand rather than judge or fix.

This has deepened all my relationships, not just my marriage, but my friendships, my relationship with my daughter, even my interactions with acquaintances and coworkers. People can sense when you're genuinely trying to understand them versus just waiting for your turn to talk.

My daughter told me she feels comfortable telling me about her struggles because she knows I won't rush into problem-solving mode. "You actually want to understand what I'm going through," she said, "not just make it go away so you feel better."

That feedback meant everything to me because it told me I'd finally learned to offer what I'd always wanted to give: genuine understanding and support, after years of getting it wrong.

Empathy in Daily Life

The most important empathy practice I've found is simply slowing down enough to really see the people around you. We're all so busy, so caught up in our own mental chatter, that we often miss what's happening with the people we care about most.

II've also learned to pay attention to my own emotional state as it affects my capacity for empathy. When I'm stressed, tired, or overwhelmed, I'm much less able to tune into other people's needs. Recognizing this helps me either take care of my own emotional state first or at least acknowledge to others that I might not be as present as I'd like to be.

Learning Through Experience

My understanding of empathy has evolved through my two marriages. In my first marriage, I was so focused on protecting myself emotionally that I had little capacity for truly understanding my partner's experience. Every conversation felt like a potential threat, so I was always in defensive mode.

In my current marriage, I've learned that empathy creates more safety, not less. When we both feel understood, there's less need for defensiveness. We can disagree about things without it feeling like a rejection of who we are as people.

This shift didn't happen overnight. It took years of consciously choosing understanding over being right, curiosity over judgment, presence over distraction. But the payoff has been a relationship where both of us feel seen and valued for who we are, not who we think we should be.

The Gift of Being Understood

Learning to empathize has made my relationships richer and more satisfying, but it's also made me a happier person. There's something fulfilling about connecting with another person's experience, about making someone feel seen and understood.

And the more empathy I've shown to others, the more I've received in return. My husband has become much better at tuning into my emotional needs as I've gotten better at tuning into his. My daughter shares more with me because she trusts that I'll try to understand her perspective.

Empathy creates a positive cycle in relationships: the more understanding you offer, the more safe and connected everyone feels, which creates even more opportunities for authentic sharing and deeper connection.

It's not always easy, sometimes sitting with someone else's pain or confusion is uncomfortable. But it's some of the most important work we can do in our relationships, because feeling understood is one of the deepest human needs we all share.

What's resonated most with you so far?

I hope you're enjoying *The Relationship Code for Couples* and finding real, practical ways to strengthen your connection and communication.

Whether it's been a helpful tool, a case study that felt familiar, or just a reminder that you're not alone, if something has stuck with you, I'd love to know.

 Please take a moment to leave a quick review. Your feedback helps me continue creating resources like this, and it encourages other couples to start their own journey toward a stronger, happier relationship.

Click on the link here

or scan the QR code

Mindful Communication

My husband and I were having dinner at a restaurant last month when I noticed the couple at the table next to us. They'd been there for over an hour, but I hadn't heard them exchange more than a few words. Both were absorbed in their phones, occasionally showing each other something on their screens, but never actually talking.

It struck me how easily that could be us on a busy week when we're both stressed and distracted. The difference between being together and actually being present with each other.

That observation made me think about how much our constantly connected world challenges our ability to have real conversations. We're always partially somewhere else, checking notifications, thinking about the next thing on our to-do list, or mentally rehearsing conversations we need to have with other people.

The Challenge of Single-Tasking

Learning to be fully present during conversations has been one of the hardest skills for me to develop, mainly because it goes against everything our culture tells us about productivity and efficiency.

I spent years thinking that multitasking during conversations was smart time management. I could have a discussion with my husband while folding laundry, answer my daughter's questions while checking work emails, or catch up with friends while tidying the house.

The problem was that nobody ever felt like they had my full attention, and I wasn't retaining much from any of these interactions. I was managing multiple inputs but not really connecting with anyone.

The shift came when I started noticing how different I felt when someone gave me their complete attention versus when they were clearly doing other things while we talked. Complete attention felt like a gift, rare and valuable. Divided attention felt dismissive, even when I knew the person cared about me.

Creating Sacred Space

Now I try to create what I think of as "sacred space" for important conversations. Not sacred in a religious sense, but sacred in the sense that this time and attention is set apart from everything else competing for my focus.

This means eliminating distractions before the conversation starts. I put my phone in another room, close my laptop, even clear physical clutter from the space if that helps me focus. It's become a small ritual that signals to both me and the other person that this conversation matters.

The physical environment makes a bigger difference than I expected. When the space feels calm and uncluttered, my mind follows suit. When there are visual distractions everywhere, part of my brain stays engaged with managing or organizing instead of listening.

My husband and I discovered that our best conversations happen during walks together. Something about the gentle, rhythmic movement, and the fact that we're not making intense eye contact makes it easier to share difficult things. The walking seems to calm both our nervous systems.

Diane's Story:

Diane, a woman in her 60s from the U.S., has been in a long-term relationship for over a decade. When asked how she and her partner communicate, her answer is refreshingly real: "Pretty good, we have our moments."

For her, being emotionally open and honest comes naturally. She feels heard when she speaks, and when disagreements come up, they talk things out. While conversations about emotional needs happen only occasionally, she describes their communication styles as "very similar" and her own as "open and expressive." It's clear they share a comfort with each other that allows for directness without drama.

They haven't explored love languages, and Diane admitted she wasn't familiar with the concept. But she knows what works for them: "Just say it." No elaborate systems, no overthinking, just honest, straightforward communication.

The times she feels most connected to her partner are simple too. Being together with their daughter brings a natural sense of closeness. There hasn't been a big breakthrough moment in how they communicate, and maybe that's because they haven't needed one. No major trust to rebuild, no major shifts, just a steady rhythm.

Her biggest recurring issue? "Snoring." And when asked what advice she'd offer other couples, her message is plain and powerful: "Just keep talking."

My thoughts:

Diane's responses are simple, but don't let that simplicity fool you. There's strength in it. Her relationship is built on honesty, familiarity, and the steady communication that doesn't need a breakthrough to be effective. "Just say it" and "just keep talking" might sound casual, but they hold wisdom that's easy to overlook. It's a reminder that strong communication doesn't have to be complicated, just consistent.

Reflection Prompt:

What does "just say it" mean in your relationship? Are there moments when holding back causes more tension than speaking up? How might honest, low-pressure communication look for you and your partner?

The Practice of Emotional Regulation

Mindful communication isn't just about paying attention, it's about managing your own emotional state so you can stay present even when conversations get difficult.

I learned this during a tense discussion about my mother-in-law's care. I could feel myself getting defensive and reactive, my heart rate increasing, my thoughts becoming scattered. In the past, I would have either shut down or said something I'd regret later.

I asked for a two-minute break to collect myself. I went to the bathroom, took several slow, deep breaths, and reminded myself that we were both trying to do the right thing, even if we disagreed about what that meant.

When I came back, I could engage with the conversation instead of my emotional reaction to the conversation. We found a solution that worked for both of us, something that wouldn't have been possible if I'd stayed in reactive mode.

Now I recognize the early signs that I'm getting overwhelmed and reactive, tension in my shoulders, shallow breathing, the urge to interrupt or defend. When I notice these signals, I can pause and collect myself before continuing.

The Quality of Attention

There's a difference between hearing words and receiving communication. When I'm paying full attention, I notice not just what someone is saying but how they're saying it, their tone, their energy, what they're not saying.

This became clear during a conversation with my daughter about her job search. On the surface, she was giving me updates about applications and interviews. But when I tuned in, I could hear the anxiety underneath her matter-of-fact tone, the self-doubt she wasn't expressing.

Instead of just responding to the information she was sharing, I could address what she was going through: "This process sounds stressful. How are you taking care of yourself through all this uncertainty?"

That shift from surface to depth transformed our conversation. She felt seen in a way that wouldn't have happened if I'd just been tracking the logistics of her job search.

Technology and Presence

One of the biggest challenges to mindful communication in modern relationships is our relationship with technology. It's not just that phones and computers distract us during conversations, they rewire our brains to expect constant stimulation and instant responses.

I had to retrain my attention span for conversation. I noticed that after periods of heavy screen time, I'd become impatient during slower, more reflective discussions. My brain wanted the quick dopamine hits of notifications and updates, not the slower satisfaction of deep human connection.

Creating phone-free zones has been crucial. Not just putting devices on silent, but removing them from the space. Even when my phone is face-down on the table, part of my attention is monitoring for the light or vibration that signals a new message.

My husband and I now leave our phones in the kitchen during evening conversations in the living room. It felt awkward at first, like we were missing a limb, but now those phone-free conversations are some of our most connecting times.

Staying Grounded During Conflict

The real test of mindful communication comes during disagreements. When emotions are high, my natural tendency is to either shut down or become reactive. Neither of these states allows for productive dialogue.

I've learned to use my breath as an anchor during difficult conversations. When I feel myself getting triggered, I focus on breathing slowly and deeply while continuing to listen. This keeps my nervous system regulated enough to stay engaged instead of going into fight-or-flight mode.

During one argument about household responsibilities, I felt that familiar surge of defensiveness when my husband expressed frustration about something I'd forgotten to do. Instead of immediately explaining why I'd been overwhelmed, I took three slow breaths and really listened to what he was saying.

I realized he wasn't attacking me—he was expressing that he felt unsupported. Once I could hear that underneath his frustration, I could respond to his actual need instead of defending against what I thought was criticism.

The Ripple Effects

When you consistently bring mindful presence to your conversations, it changes not just what you say, but how others feel in your presence. People relax when they sense that you're fully there with them. They're more willing to be vulnerable, more likely to share what's really going on.

My relationships have deepened as I've developed this practice. Not because I've become a perfect communicator, but because people feel received when they talk to me. They know I'm not somewhere else mentally, not waiting for my turn to talk, not judging what they're sharing.

The practice has also made me more aware of when I'm not present. I can feel the difference now between conversations where I'm truly engaged and ones where I'm going through the motions. That awareness allows me to course-correct in the moment.

Simple Daily Practices

Mindful communication doesn't require hours of meditation or complex techniques. It's built through small, consistent practices:

Before important conversations, I take a few conscious breaths and set an intention to be present. During phone calls, I close my eyes or look out the window instead of multitasking. When someone is sharing something important, I repeat key phrases silently to help my attention stay anchored on their words.

These aren't grand gestures, they're tiny choices to prioritize presence over productivity, connection over efficiency. But the cumulative effect has been transformative, both for my relationships and for my sense of calm and centeredness.

The practice of mindful communication has taught me that attention is one of the most precious gifts we can offer each other. In a world full of distractions, choosing to be fully present with someone is an act of love.

The Ripple Effects of Presence

When you consistently show up fully present in conversations, people share more meaningful things with you. My daughter has come to me with bigger concerns because she knows I'll give her my complete attention. My friends call when they need to talk through serious situations because they trust that I'll really listen.

This isn't about being perfect. I still get distracted, still catch my mind wandering. But the intention to be present, and the practice of returning my attention when it drifts, has transformed the quality of my relationships.

My husband told me he feels more connected to me now than in the early years of our marriage, and I think this practice of mindful communication is a big part of why. When someone feels truly seen and heard by you, it creates a safety and intimacy that goes far beyond just getting along well.

Simple Daily Practices

I've developed some simple habits that help me stay present during everyday conversations:

Before important discussions, I take three deep breaths and set an intention to really listen. During phone calls, I do nothing else, no checking email, no tidying up, just focusing on the conversation. When my daughter wants to talk, I stop what I'm doing and give her my full attention, even if it's just for five minutes.

These aren't elaborate mindfulness practices, they're just small ways of choosing presence over distraction. But the cumulative effect has been remarkable. Conversations feel richer, misunderstandings happen less often, and the people I care about feel more valued and heard.

The Gift of Your Attention

Understand that giving someone your full attention is one of the most loving things you can do. In a world full of distractions and competing demands, choosing to be present with another person is a profound gift.

It doesn't require special skills or training, just the willingness to put everything else aside and be with someone. But the impact on your relationships can be transformative.

When you're truly present during conversations, you're not just exchanging information, you're creating a connection. You're showing the other person that they matter enough for you to give them your complete attention. And that kind of presence becomes the foundation for all the deeper communication skills we've been exploring throughout this book.

The practice of mindful communication has taught me that love isn't just what you say, it's how you listen. And when you learn to listen with your whole being, everything else about your relationships shifts in beautiful ways.

Addressing Common Pain-Points

I used to think I was pretty good at reading between the lines. You know when you walk away from a conversation thinking everything went well, only to discover later that your partner is upset about something you said or didn't say? I've been there more times than I care to admit.

Just last month, my husband mentioned he was tired after work, and I suggested we order takeout instead of cooking. Seemed helpful to me. Later that evening, I learned he had anticipated cooking together all day, his preferred method of relaxation. My "helpful" suggestion felt like a rejection to him. Who knew?

These kinds of mix-ups happen to all of us, and I've learned they usually come from the stories we tell ourselves about what people mean. When someone seems short with us, we might assume they're annoyed with us, when really they're just overwhelmed by their day. I've noticed this pattern in my own relationships over the years. In my first marriage, I internalized everything. If my ex-husband was quiet during dinner, I'd assume I'd done something wrong, when often he was just processing work stress.

I've also seen how our past can color everything. After my divorce, I carried a lot of baggage into my current marriage. When my husband would come home late without calling, my mind would jump to all sorts of conclusions based on past hurts rather than trusting what I knew about him. It took time and a lot of honest conversations to recognize when I was reacting to old wounds rather than what was actually happening.

The thing I've learned about expressing feelings is that it's harder than it sounds. Those "I" statements we talked about in Chapter 4, they really help. But beyond that, I've found it's worth checking if your message landed the way you meant it. I'll sometimes ask my husband, "What did you hear me say?" It might sound awkward at first, but it's saved us from so many unnecessary arguments.

One thing that's made a real difference in our marriage is those morning coffee chats I mentioned before. We don't have formal "check-ins" or anything that is scheduled, but we make time to talk about what's going on in our heads. Sometimes it's just five minutes before the day gets crazy, but it helps us stay connected to each other's inner world.

I've learned it's better to ask questions when something feels off rather than letting my imagination run wild. "Hey, you seem quiet tonight, everything okay?" works so much better than stewing about what I might have done wrong.

Exercise: Building Intentional Clarity

Try this with your partner: pick something you need to discuss, maybe weekend plans or how to handle a family situation. Take turns explaining your perspective, but here's the twist: the other person has to repeat back what they heard before responding. It sounds silly, but it's amazing how often we think we're saying one thing while our partner hears something completely different.

After important conversations, I've gotten into the habit of jotting down a few notes about how things went. Not formally, just quick thoughts about where we understood each other well and where things got murky. It's helped me recognize my own patterns, like how I tend to be vague when I'm worried about conflict.

Communication is like learning to dance together. Some days we're in perfect step, other days someone's stepping on toes. The goal isn't to never have misunderstandings, it's to get better at working through them when they happen.

Victoria & James's Story:

Victoria (55) and James (57) from the UK have been married for over a decade. When asked how they usually communicate, they both gave the same answer: "It's a work in progress." That theme carries through much of their story.

When it comes to feeling heard, both say it happens rarely. Their conflict styles also differ: James shared that they talk it out, argue then cool off, and sometimes one of them "wins" the disagreement. Victoria, on the other hand, says they often withdraw or avoid the topic altogether. It's clear they don't always meet in the middle, but they're still showing up and trying.

Victoria said she's emotionally open depending on the situation, while James feels safe being vulnerable. He says they talk about emotional needs regularly, while she says only occasionally. These kinds of gaps are common in long-term relationships, especially when each partner communicates in different ways. Victoria tends to keep things to herself; James describes himself as open and expressive. Together, they agree their styles are "a bit different."

They've talked about love languages, but haven't put them into practice. And yet, they've found things that work: "resolving issues and agreeing to a way forward" has helped them navigate conflict. Their biggest challenge? "Inability to focus on each other's point of view." But even there, they've seen some growth. A difficult situation involving money became a turning point, one that led them to start being more open and honest with each other.

When asked when they last felt truly connected, they pointed to physical intimacy as a space where closeness still comes naturally. Their advice to other couples reflects their experience: "Just keep talking. Be nice to one another. And forgive the little things."

My thoughts:

This couple is living in the space between knowing they love each other and still learning how to communicate that. Their willingness to keep working on it, even when things feel mismatched, shows strength. Not every couple starts on the same page, but what matters is that they're still writing the story together.

Reflection Prompt:

What's one small way you and your partner could better focus on each other's point of view? Are there specific situations where listening feels harder, and how could you shift that dynamic?

When We Stop Really Seeing Each Other

There's something heartbreaking about sitting next to someone you love and feeling like they're a million miles away. I remember going through a phase in my current marriage where we'd sit on the couch together, both on our phones, barely talking. We were physically there but emotionally checked out. It's one of those things that happens so gradually you don't notice until one day you realize you feel lonely even when you're together.

I've noticed this disconnect often starts small. Maybe one partner shares exciting news and gets a distracted "that's nice" in response. Or those little touches that used to happen, a hand on the shoulder, a quick kiss, start becoming rare. Eye contact during conversations begins to feel forced rather than natural. Before you know it, you're living parallel lives under the same roof.

In my experience, this kind of emotional distance usually has roots. Stress is a big one. When my husband was going through a challenging time at work, he'd come home so drained that engaging felt impossible for him. I took it to heart at first, thinking he was pulling away from me. It took honest conversation to understand he was just trying to survive his days.

Unresolved issues are another culprit. I learned this the hard way in my first marriage. When we'd have an argument and sweep it under the rug without resolving it, it created this invisible wall between us. Those buried resentments have a way of poisoning the atmosphere, making genuine connection feel risky or fake.

Life changes can throw us off balance, too. When we moved to a new city early in my current marriage, both of us were dealing with so much change that we forgot to adjust to each other. We were so focused on settling in that we stopped nurturing our connection.

I've found that getting back to each other requires being intentional about it. For us, it started with simple things, like putting our phones in another room during dinner, planning one activity we could do together each weekend, even if it was just a walk around the neighborhood. The key was creating new shared experiences rather than just falling into our separate routines.

One thing that's helped us is having a Sunday morning ritual where we sit with coffee and just check in with each other about the week ahead. Nothing formal, just a chance to make sure we're on the same page and feeling connected before Monday hits.

Activities That Bring You Back Together

I'm not talking about elaborate date nights here, though those have their place. Sometimes it's as simple as cooking dinner together instead of taking turns, or finding a TV show you both want to watch. The point is doing something that requires you to be present with each other.

My husband and I started doing what we call "highs and lows" most evenings, just sharing the best and worst parts of our day. It sounds basic, but it keeps us tuned into each other's inner world. Some nights it's deep, other nights it's just "the coffee machine broke and my meeting went well," but it keeps that connection thread strong.

One practice that surprised me with how much it helped was taking five minutes before bed to just sit together quietly. No phones, no TV, just being in the same space. We don't always talk, but there's something powerful about choosing to be present with each other.

Listening When Life Gets Loud

We've all been there - trying to have an important conversation while the kids are fighting, phones are buzzing, and life is happening all around you.

I used to think I was a good multitasker, that I could listen to my husband while scrolling through my phone or folding laundry. Turns out, I wasn't fooling anyone, least of all him. There's a difference between hearing words and listening, and it shows.

The hardest part for me was admitting how often I was only half-present during conversations. I'd be nodding along while mentally writing my grocery list or worrying about a work deadline. My husband would finish talking, and I'd realize I didn't know what he'd said. Not exactly the foundation for meaningful communication.

I've learned that real listening requires boundaries. We had to get serious about phone-free time, especially during important conversations. It felt weird at first, like we were missing out on something urgent. But nothing was ever as urgent as we thought, and our conversations got so much deeper when we weren't competing with screens.

We also created what I call our "talk spot", a corner of the living room where we sit when we need to discuss something important. It's nothing fancy, just two comfortable chairs facing each other. But having that designated space helps us both shift into listening mode.

When I'm struggling to stay focused, I've found that taking a few deep breaths before we talk helps center me. It's like hitting a reset button on my scattered brain. Sometimes I'll also put my hands in my lap or hold a cup of tea, something to keep my body still so my mind can follow.

Exercises for Better Listening

One thing we practice is taking turns talking for three minutes straight without interruption. The listening partner can't jump in with questions or comments, just has to absorb what's being said. It's harder than it sounds, especially when you disagree with something or want to clarify a point. But it's amazing how much more you hear when you're not preparing your rebuttal. It made me realise I was a poor listener.

After important conversations, we'll check in with each other about how well we felt heard. It's not about scoring points or finding fault, it's about getting better at this together. Sometimes my husband will say, "I felt like you were somewhere else during that conversation," and instead of getting defensive, I try to acknowledge it and figure out what pulled my attention away.

The truth is, listening well in our noisy world takes practice and intention. Some days I'm better at it than others. But when I give my full attention to my husband during a conversation, I can see the difference it makes. He relaxes, opens up more, and we both walk away feeling more connected.

Try This:

For the next 24 hours, be intentional about your listening. Put your phone away during conversations, make eye contact, and resist the urge to interrupt. Check in with yourself: Did your partner respond differently? Did you feel more connected?

The goal isn't perfection, it's progress. Every time we choose to listen, we're choosing our relationship over the distractions. And that choice, made over and over, is what builds the connection we all want.

Aligning Communication Styles

I've talked before about how roles can become unbalanced in relationships, especially around emotional labor and household responsibilities. But there's another layer to this that's worth exploring, how the way we communicate can sometimes reinforce these imbalances or create new ones.

A simple conversation about weekend plans turned into our biggest fight last month, and I couldn't figure out how it had happened. We'd started by discussing whether to visit my sister or stay home, and somehow ended up arguing about respect and consideration and who makes decisions in our relationship.

It wasn't until later that I realized the real issue: my husband and I approach conversations completely differently.

I'm someone who likes to think things through before I speak. I'll mull over ideas, consider different angles, and then present what feels like a well-thought-out plan. My husband thinks out loud. He'll start talking through an idea while it's still half-formed, working through the details as he goes. For years, this drove me crazy. I'd hear his initial thoughts and think that was his final decision, then get frustrated when he'd change direction mid-conversation.

It took me way too long to realize that neither of us were wrong, we just process information differently. Once I understood that his "thinking out loud" wasn't indecision, but how he works through problems, our conversations got so much smoother.

When Different Styles Work Together

I think of communication styles like different instruments in a band. Each one brings something unique to the music, and when they work together, the result is richer than any single instrument could create alone.

My sister and her husband are a perfect example of this. She's very direct and gets straight to the point, while he's more diplomatic and considers everyone's feelings before speaking. Early in their marriage, she thought he was being evasive, and he thought she was being harsh. But over time, they've learned to appreciate what each brings. Her directness helps them address issues swiftly, while his diplomacy helps them do it without hurt feelings.

I've noticed that the key is respecting each other's natural way of communicating rather than trying to change it. In my first marriage, I spent a lot of energy trying to get my ex-husband to communicate more like me. It was exhausting and ultimately futile. In my current marriage, I've learned to work with our differences instead of against them. Maybe age brings wisdom.

When both people feel like their communication style is valued, something beautiful happens. You stop defending your approach and start being curious about your partner's. The tension that comes from feeling misunderstood fades, and you see how your different styles can complement each other.

I've found that understanding each other's strengths makes an enormous difference. My husband is great at big-picture thinking and seeing possibilities I might miss. I'm better at working through practical details and potential problems. When we combine those strengths, we make better decisions together.

We've learned to work with our differences instead of against them. When we're planning something important, like a family vacation, I handle the research and logistics while he focuses on the fun activities and experiences we want to have. We each contribute what we're good at, which works so much better than forcing ourselves to approach everything the same way.

Exercise: Joint Storytelling

Here's something fun we tried that helped us understand how our styles work together. We decided to make up a story together, taking turns adding sentences. I started with, "Once upon a time, there was a couple who planned to build their dream house." Then he added a sentence, then me, and so on.

What was fascinating was watching how our different approaches showed up even in something silly like making up a story. I added practical details and move the plot forward logically, while he added creative twists and emotional depth. Neither approach was better. They just created a richer story together than either of us could have told alone. I must admit, it got a bit silly at times, but fun.

Try this with your partner. Pick any simple story starter and take turns building on it. Pay attention to how you each contribute differently, and talk about what you notice afterward.

Working as a Team

The biggest shift in my communication happened when I stopped thinking about conversations as something I had to navigate alone and started seeing them as collaborative projects. Instead of trying to convince my husband of my point of view, I began approaching our talks as opportunities to build something together.

This showed up most clearly when we were house-hunting a few years ago. At first, we were approaching it like we each had our own agenda to push. I was focused on practical considerations like commute times and school districts, while he was drawn to character and potential. We were talking past each other and getting frustrated.

Then we had this lightbulb moment where we realized we were both trying to find a home we'd love. We just had different priorities or ideas of what that meant. So we sat down and talked about what "home" meant to each of us. It turned out we wanted a lot of the same things; we were just using different words to describe them.

From that point on, we approached each house viewing as a team. Instead of hoping the other person would come around to our preference, we'd walk through together and talk about how the space felt to both of us. We found a house that met both our practical needs and felt like a place where we could build the life we wanted.

Charles & Sharon's Story:

> Charles (55) and Sharon (52), a married couple from the UK, have been together for over 20 years. When asked how they communicate, their answer is honest and straightforward: "We struggle to connect."

They say they "sometimes" feel heard, and when conflict arises, their usual pattern is to argue, then cool off. Emotional honesty doesn't come easily; it "depends on the situation." Conversations about emotional needs are rare. Trust hasn't been broken, but communication hasn't quite found its footing either.

Their styles differ—Sharon shared she tends to avoid conflict, and they both described their communication approaches as "totally different." They aren't familiar with love languages and didn't point to anything specific that works well for them when it comes to communication. They also chose not to name a recurring challenge or give advice to others.

And yet, when asked when they last felt truly connected, the answer was: "Always." That single word says a lot. It suggests that despite their communication struggles, there's still something solid and enduring between them, a sense of closeness that's woven into their daily life.

There hasn't been a breakthrough moment in how they communicate. No big turning point. But that they're willing to name the difficulty out loud, and take part in a survey like this, might just be a sign that they're still trying.

My thoughts:

Charles and Sharon's responses are quietly powerful, even in what's left unsaid. There's a clear sense of emotional distance and complexity in their dynamic, but also glimpses of connection ("always" feeling close, despite communication struggles). That contrast makes this an especially valuable and relatable case study.

Reflection Prompt:

Is there a difference between feeling close and communicating well in your relationship? What's one small step you could take to strengthen both at the same time?

Creating Your Communication Mission Statement

One thing that's helped us stay aligned is having a conversation about what we want our communication to feel like. We've talked about wanting our conversations to feel honest, respectful, and safe, even when we're discussing difficult topics.

Having that shared understanding gives us something to aim for when emotions are running high. When we're in the middle of a tense conversation, I can remember that we both want this to feel respectful, and it helps me choose my words more carefully.

We've also learned to switch roles sometimes. If I'm usually the one who brings up difficult topics, we'll have him initiate a conversation about something sensitive. If he typically takes the lead on planning, I'll step up and guide that discussion. It's been eye-opening to experience communication from the other person's perspective.

When we're facing a problem together, we've gotten better at brainstorming as a team rather than each of us coming up with our own solution and then trying to convince the other. We sit down with a piece of paper and write out all the options we can think of, then talk through the pros and cons together. It sounds formal, but it feels more collaborative and creative than our old way of approaching problems.

One practical thing we've developed is our own shorthand for emotions. We have specific words and phrases that mean something particular to us. Like when I say I'm "feeling spiky," he knows I'm overwhelmed and need some space to think before we continue talking. When he says he's "in planning mode," I know he needs to work through all the details out loud before we make any decisions.

The goal isn't to communicate exactly the same way, it's to understand each other's way well enough that we can work together effectively. Some of our best solutions have come from combining our different approaches rather than trying to find one approach that works for both of us.

Activities to Practice Collaboration

One thing we did that was helpful was tackle a project together that required us to coordinate our efforts. We reorganized our garage, which sounds mundane but required us to make a lot of decisions together, share responsibilities, and communicate constantly about what we were doing.

Another project that brought us closer was creating our 'vision board', a collection of pictures and ideas representing things we want to do together in the future. We each contributed our own ideas, and then we talked about which ones excited both of us and how we might make them happen.

Learning to work with someone else's communication style is an ongoing process. Some days we nail it, and some days we miss the mark completely. But the effort to understand and appreciate each other's way of communicating has made our relationship feel more like a true partnership. We're not trying to change each other anymore, we're trying to build something together that honors both of us.

When Old Patterns Get in the Way

I grew up watching my parents' marriage, where my father made most of the big decisions and my mother kept her opinions to herself unless asked. It wasn't that she didn't have thoughts. She was very smart and insightful, but that was just how things worked in their generation. Without realizing it, I carried some of those patterns into my own relationships.

After my divorce, I was determined not to lose myself again in a relationship. But I over corrected, I became defensive about everything, insisting on having equal input even when it didn't matter. I was so afraid of disappearing that I exhausted myself trying to prove I had strong opinions about every little decision.

I've learned that it's not about keeping score of who talks more or who gets their way. It's about both people feeling like their thoughts and feelings matter. In my current marriage, we've had to work at this. My husband grew up in a family where the loudest voice won, so his instinct is to jump in and state his opinion about everything. I still need time to think things through first. We've had to learn to make space for both approaches.

Making Sure Both Voices Matter

There's something beautiful about a conversation where both people walk away feeling heard. It doesn't mean you agree about everything, but it means you both feel like your perspective was valued and considered.

I've noticed this happens most naturally when we're both genuinely curious about each other's point of view. Instead of waiting for my turn to talk, I try to understand why my husband sees things the way he does. When he feels heard and understood, he becomes more curious about my perspective, too.

The conversations that go sideways are usually the ones where we're both so focused on being right that we stop listening. I'll catch myself preparing my counterargument while he's still talking, or he'll interrupt me because he's eager to share his viewpoint. Those conversations leave us both feeling frustrated and misunderstood.

We've learned some simple practices that help keep things balanced. We'll sometimes take turns, one person shares their thoughts before the other responds. It sounds formal, but it helps both of us feel less rushed and more thorough in what we're saying.

I've also started asking more open-ended questions instead of leading ones. Instead of "Don't you think we should...?" I'll ask "What's your take on this?" or "How do you see this playing out?" It invites him to share his thoughts rather than just react to mine.

Try This: The Equal Voice Check-In

Once a week, sit down with your partner and each share one thing you've been thinking about but haven't brought up yet. It could be anything, a work situation, something about your relationship, a family issue, or even just something you've been curious about. Take turns sharing without jumping into problem-solving or advice-giving. Just listen and ask questions to understand better.

We also started what we call "co-authoring" our bigger decisions. When we were deciding whether to renovate our kitchen, we each made a list of what we wanted and what we were worried about. Then we sat down and created one combined list that represented both of our priorities. It helped us see where we were aligned and where we needed to negotiate.

Learning from Each Other's Backgrounds

My husband comes from a family that's much more emotionally expressive than mine. They hug a lot, interrupt each other constantly, and say exactly what they're thinking the moment they think it. When I first experienced a family dinner at his parents' house, I was overwhelmed. Everyone was talking at once, laughing loudly, and debating everything from politics to the best way to cook pasta.

Coming from a family where we spoke in turns and kept our voices down, I initially interpreted all that energy as chaos or even conflict. It took time for me to understand that this was how they showed love and engagement. Their interruptions weren't rude, they were excited. Their debates weren't fights, they were how they connected. We lived in Spain for years (in fact it's where we met), now the Spanish are certainly expressive and loud. I used to think everyone was falling out with each-other.

Meanwhile, my husband had to learn that when I am quiet during family gatherings, it doesn't mean I'm upset or judging anyone. I'm just processing all the stimulation and figuring out how to join in. What looks like withdrawal to him is me finding my footing.

We've had to translate between our different family cultures constantly. When I need time to think before responding to something important, he's learned not to interpret that as rejection or disinterest. When he thinks out loud and changes his mind three times in one conversation, I've learned not to get frustrated with what seems like indecisiveness.

One thing that's been fun is sharing traditions from our different backgrounds. I introduced him to my family's very quiet, contemplative Christmas morning routine, and he introduced me to his family's tradition of everyone talking at once during holiday meals. We've created our own blend that feels comfortable for both of us.

I've learned so much about different ways of communicating just by paying attention to the surrounding couples. My neighbor grew up in a family where disagreement was disrespectful, so she struggles to voice different opinions even in healthy situations. My friend's husband comes from a culture where men and women communicate differently with each other than they do with same-gender friends, which has required some navigation in their marriage.

The key, I've found is being curious rather than judgmental about these differences. Instead of thinking "Why does he always...?" I try to wonder "What's behind this pattern?" Understanding where someone's communication style comes from helps me respond to the person rather than just react to the behavior.

Activities to Bridge Different Backgrounds

One thing that's brought us closer is cooking meals from each other's family traditions. It sounds simple, but there's something powerful about learning to make someone's comfort food. We talk about memories and family stories while we cook, and I get to understand what "home" feels like to him.

We've also started what we call "culture sharing" evenings where we'll watch a movie or read something that's important to one of our backgrounds and then talk about it afterward. It's not formal or educational, more like show-and-tell for adults.

The goal isn't to become the same or to erase our differences. It's to understand each other well enough that our different styles become strengths rather than sources of confusion. When we can appreciate why someone approaches communication the way they do, it's easier to work with that style rather than against it.

Progressive Communication Approaches

Last chapter, I talked about how old patterns from our upbringing can shape who speaks up and who stays quiet in relationships. But I want to dig deeper into something that's been on my mind since my divorce, how some of these patterns aren't just personal, they're cultural, passed down through generations like family recipes that maybe don't taste as good as they used to.

I had dinner with my husband, and we started discussing who would handle some weekend tasks. I deferred to his preferences, even though I had strong opinions about how things should be done. It hit me later that I was falling back into this old script where the man's voice somehow carried more weight, not because he intended it that way, but because that's just how I'd seen it done growing up.

My grandmother rarely spoke up during family decisions. My mother was a bit more vocal but still deferred to my father on "important" matters. I inherited these invisible rules about whose voice mattered when, and it took years for me to recognize how they were affecting my relationships.

In my first marriage, I rarely challenged my ex-husband's decisions about money or major life changes. I told myself I was being supportive, but I was just following this unspoken script that said his judgment was more important than mine. When I finally started speaking up more, he seemed relieved, turned out he'd been feeling pressure to make all the decisions alone.

Recognizing the Scripts We're Following

The thing about these inherited communication patterns is they're often invisible until you look for them. I've noticed them in couples around me too. My friend Sarah handles all the social planning and emotional conversations in her marriage, while her husband takes charge of financial discussions and household repairs. They're both intelligent, capable people, but they've somehow divided the world of communication into his and hers.

Some of these patterns made sense in our parents' or grandparents' generations, but they can create genuine problems now. When one person dominates conversations, the other's thoughts and feelings can get buried. I've seen marriages where one partner becomes the "quiet one" not because they don't have opinions, but because they've gotten out of practice expressing them.

The emotional cost of this is real. I remember feeling frustrated in my first marriage but not being able to put my finger on why. I felt like I was disappearing, but I couldn't explain it because, technically, we weren't fighting. We just weren't both fully present in our conversations.

After my divorce, I had to learn how to have a voice again. It was like exercising muscles I hadn't used in years. At first, I over-corrected; I became defensive about every little thing because I was so afraid of going back to being invisible. I had to find the middle ground between doormat and bulldozer.

Building New Habits Together

The good news is these patterns can change, but it takes intentional effort from both people. My current husband and I have had to work at this. We came from families with very different communication styles, and we've had to create our own approach that works for both of us.

We do regular check-ins about how balanced our conversations feel. Not in a formal way, but just occasionally asking each other, "How are we doing with this? Do you feel heard?" It's amazing how often one of us will admit to holding back or taking over more than we realized.

I mentioned in Chapter 15 how we've learned to appreciate each other's different communication styles. But beyond working with our natural differences, we've also had to unlearn some of the automatic patterns we inherited about whose voice should take priority when.

When Both Voices Matter

There's something powerful about a conversation where both people walk away feeling like their perspective was valued. It doesn't mean you agree about everything, but it means you both feel like equals in the discussion.

I've noticed this happens most naturally when we approach conversations as problem-solving partners rather than adversaries. Instead of one person making a case and the other person responding, we're both exploring the issue together. When my husband feels truly heard and understood, he naturally becomes more curious about my perspective, too.

The conversations that go sideways are usually the ones where we fall back into old scripts, where one of us assumes they should lead, or the other defers. Those conversations leave us both feeling disconnected, even if we reach a decision.

Some practical things that have helped us stay balanced: We take turns sharing our thoughts before the other responds. We ask open-ended questions instead of leading ones. We've learned to notice when one of us is dominating the conversation and reset.

One exercise that's been helpful is what we call "equal input" decision-making. When we're planning something important, like a vacation or a home improvement project, we each make our own list of priorities and concerns first. Then we sit down together and create one combined list that represents both of our perspectives. It ensures both voices are part of the foundation, not just the finishing touches. We enjoy doing this when we choose which excursions to go on. I print out the list available. Cross off the ones I know neither of us would be interested in, then we both score them with 1,2 or 3 stars. 3 star ones are booked, then we move on and eliminate the least popular ones. It's fun.

Learning from Each Other's Worlds

Beyond breaking free from inherited scripts, there's another layer to this, learning to appreciate and work with the different worlds we each come from. I think this is one of the most important aspects of building a relationship where both people feel valued.

My husband comes from a family where emotions are expressed very openly. When someone is upset, hurt, or excited, everyone knows about it right away. My family was much more reserved. We processed feelings privately first and only shared them, if it seemed necessary.

Neither approach is wrong, but they can create misunderstandings if you don't understand where they come from. When I go quiet during a difficult conversation, my husband used to think I was shutting down or pulling away. When he would express frustration and emotion, I used to think he was being dramatic or losing control.

We've had to learn each other's emotional languages. Now when I say I need time to think about something, he understands I'm processing, not avoiding. When he expresses his feelings right away, I understand he's sharing, not attacking.

We've also discovered some beautiful ways to bridge our different backgrounds. I've learned to share my thoughts and feelings more immediately, which feels scary but also freeing. He's learned to pause and consider before expressing emotions, which helps me feel safer in difficult conversations.

Activities That Build Understanding

One thing that's brought us closer is learning about each other's family communication patterns. We'll talk about how certain topics were discussed in our families growing up, what was appropriate to share, and what subjects were off-limits.

These conversations have helped me understand why certain things feel natural or uncomfortable for each of us. They've also helped us identify patterns we want to keep and ones we want to change.

We've also started what we call "communication experiments", trying alternative approaches to see how they feel. Sometimes I'll share a worry or an idea I have instead of processing it alone first. Sometimes he'll take time to think before responding to something emotional instead of reacting right away. I used to react to his outburst, but then I learned to leave him to blow, then return to a calmer hubby.

The goal isn't to become the same or erase our differences. It's to understand each other well enough that we can communicate in ways that feel good to both of us. When we can appreciate why someone approaches communication the way they do, it's easier to work with that style rather than against it.

Breaking free from old communication scripts is ongoing. Some days, we fall back into inherited patterns without realizing it. But the awareness itself has been transformative. We're no longer following rules we didn't choose. We're creating our own approach that honors both of our voices and backgrounds.

The most important thing I've learned is that equality in communication isn't about keeping score or making sure everything is balanced. It's about both people feeling like their thoughts, feelings, and perspectives matter. When that happens, you stop vying for airtime and start collaborating on understanding.

Overcoming Fear of Vulnerability

I still remember the first time I tried to share something personal and felt the air shift between us. My heart was pounding, my voice a little shaky, not because I didn't trust the person, but because I wasn't used to being that exposed. Vulnerability isn't something most of us grow up learning how to do. For many of us, the fear of being misunderstood, judged, or even rejected makes emotional openness feel risky. It's no wonder we hesitate, especially if we've been hurt before. But learning to face that fear is where genuine connection begins.

Fear is a powerful emotion that can hinder vulnerability, often rooted in experiences or insecurities that shape how we interact with others. Fear of rejection, for example, might stem from a time when you opened up to someone and were met with dismissal or disdain. This fear can lead to avoiding vulnerability altogether, as a protective mechanism against potential pain. Similarly, the fear of judgment might originate from instances where your honesty was met with criticism or ridicule.

These fears can become ingrained in our psyche, fueled by experiences that reinforce the belief that vulnerability equals weakness. It's crucial to recognize that these fears aren't just mental constructs but are embedded in our "primitive brain," influencing our behavior in subtle, yet profound ways.

Understanding the psychological roots of these fears involves delving into your experiences and examining how they've shaped your current communication patterns. Take some time to ponder moments when you felt exposed or vulnerable, noting any sensations or thoughts that surface.

Consider how these memories have affected your willingness to open up in your relationships. Analyzing experiences can shed light on recurring patterns, helping you recognize the triggers that prompt your fear response. For instance, if you notice a pattern of withdrawing when conversations get too personal, it may be linked to a past incident where vulnerability led to hurt or embarrassment.

The journey of confronting fear begins with gradual exposure to vulnerability in low-risk situations. This might involve expressing anxiety about an upcoming event or admitting a slight mistake. By practicing openness in these less intimidating scenarios, you can build confidence and resilience. It brings you closer while also making vulnerability feel more normal and safe between you.

Facing these fears head-on can lead to remarkable personal growth and stronger relational bonds. Embracing vulnerability allows you to break free from the constraints of fear and connect with others on a deeper level. Real-life examples abound of relationships flourishing through vulnerability. My friend Sue and her partner spent years skirting around the tough conversations, fears, frustrations, and things left unsaid. They ended up having therapy.

This helped them to reach a point where staying silent felt more uncomfortable than opening up. They revealed their insecurities. Naming fears wasn't the only step; they had to prioritize connection over comfort, which transformed their relationship. Sometimes therapy is the solution, but most relationships just need better communication.

Embracing vulnerability, though uncomfortable, can pave the way for greater trust and intimacy. When we allow ourselves to be seen without the usual filters, we create space for authenticity, mutual respect, and emotional closeness to flourish. As you embark on this journey of embracing vulnerability, remember that it's not about eliminating fear, but learning to navigate it with compassion and courage.

Recognize that fear is a natural response, but it doesn't have to dictate your actions. By acknowledging and confronting your fears, you open yourself up to a world of possibilities, greater self-awareness, deeper connections, and the potential for transformative growth. Embrace it as a gift that allows you to connect with others on a profound level, enriching your life in ways you never thought possible. As you continue this journey, may you find the courage to dive into the depths of your emotions, knowing that the rewards of vulnerability far outweigh the risks.

Building Confidence in Vulnerability

Confidence in vulnerability is a powerful thing. It starts with the realization that opening up is not a weakness, but a strength. This strength comes from self-acceptance and a deep understanding that our imperfections make us human, and therefore, relatable. When you accept yourself, flaws and all, you're more comfortable being vulnerable. This comfort stems from knowing that your worth isn't determined by others' perceptions. It's a mindset shift that transforms vulnerability into a tool for authentic connection. When you embrace this, you invite others to see the real you, fostering genuine relationships built on trust and honesty.

To cultivate this confidence, start by working on self-acceptance. Self-affirmation exercises can be beneficial here. Every morning, take a moment to stand in front of a mirror and speak words of kindness and affirmation to yourself. Remind yourself of your strengths, acknowledge your achievements, and be gentle with your shortcomings. Say things like, "I am worthy," or "I am enough," to reinforce your self-worth. This practice helps you internalize these positive beliefs, replacing self-doubt with self-confidence.

You'll also find supportive tools in the gratitude journal introduced in Chapter 3. It includes affirmations, motivational quotes, mini challenges, and ideas for rewarding yourself (which you absolutely should do). Pairing this with mindfulness practices can be especially powerful. Mindfulness encourages you to observe your thoughts and feelings without judgment. Over time, you learn to sit with discomfort and recognize it as a natural part of life. This kind of acceptance fosters self-compassion, allowing you to be kinder to yourself and more open to the idea of vulnerability.

Once you have a foundation of self-acceptance, you can practice vulnerability in safe environments. Start by sharing personal stories or emotions with someone you trust. This could be a friend, a family member, or a partner. Choose someone who has shown empathy and understanding, creating a safe space for you to express yourself. Share a memory or an experience that holds emotional significance, allowing yourself to be seen and heard. As you do this, set intentions for honesty and openness in your daily interactions. Approach conversations with a willingness to be transparent about your thoughts and feelings. When you set an intention, it helps you feel more grounded, and it signals that you're open to real connection.

Partners play a critical role in supporting each other's journey toward vulnerability. Creating a judgment-free zone is essential for fostering an environment where thoughts and feelings can be shared without fear of criticism. Encourage your partner to express themselves and listen when they do. Validate their emotions by acknowledging their experiences and responding with empathy. Expressions like "I understand why you feel that way" or "Thank you for sharing that with me" can make a significant difference. This validation reinforces the message that their vulnerability is valued, not dismissed.

Together, you and your partner can establish mutual vulnerability goals to work towards. These goals might include setting aside time each week to have open conversations or committing to sharing one personal story with each other over dinner. By working together, you create a supportive dynamic that encourages growth and strengthens your bond.

Consider incorporating a simple exercise into your routine to support these efforts. You and your partner might try a "Vulnerability Jar" where you each write down one vulnerability-related goal on a piece of paper and place it in the jar. The goals could range from "Share a childhood memory" to "Express a fear I've never talked about." Once a week, pull out a goal and work on it together.

This exercise helps you stay anchored in the practice of vulnerability, while making the experience feel more approachable and even meaningful. It serves as a reminder that vulnerability is a shared journey, one that deepens your connection and enriches your relationship.

As you continue to nurture confidence in vulnerability, remember that it's a gradual process. You won't wake up one day and feel comfortable being open. Instead, it's about taking small, consistent steps towards openness, each one building on the last. Embrace the journey, knowing that each act of vulnerability is a step towards stronger, more authentic connections.

Vulnerability isn't about being perfect; it's about being real. And in that authenticity lies the power to transform not only your relationships, but also your life. As we move forward, keep in mind that the next chapter will delve into long-term communication strategies, equipping you with tools to sustain these newfound connections and continue growing together.

Long-term Communication Strategies

A healthy relationship needs ongoing care. Without regular attention, checking in, showing appreciation, staying emotionally connected, even the strongest bond can fade. Growth keeps your connection strong, responsive, and full of possibility.

Set joint goals. They can be as simple as planning a monthly date night or as ambitious as saving for a dream vacation. By embracing change as a natural part of relationship evolution, you both allow for personal development and mutual growth. By embracing this mindset, you deepen your connection and create the kind of flexibility that helps your relationship bend, not break, when life gets messy. Fostering growth requires action, and engaging in shared experiences is a perfect start.

Consider picking up a new hobby together, like hiking or cooking. These activities inject fun and spontaneity into your routine while fostering teamwork and communication. Attending workshops or seminars focused on relationship topics can also be enlightening. They provide fresh perspectives and equip you with tools to tackle potential challenges. These shared experiences create lasting memories and strengthen your connection, laying the groundwork for a resilient and thriving relationship.

Growth is vital for relationship health, offering many benefits that contribute to long-term satisfaction. It enhances your ability to adapt to life changes, such as career shifts or family expansions, and equips you with resilience during challenging times. When both partners are committed to growth, they respond more constructively to stress, viewing obstacles as opportunities to learn and grow together. This adaptability fosters a stronger, more unified partnership, where both individuals feel supported and understood, even in the face of adversity.

To keep the momentum of growth going, consider setting and pursuing growth-oriented goals together. Creating a vision board can be a fun and inspiring way to visualize your shared aspirations.

Vision Board Exercise

Gather materials like magazines, scissors, and a board. Or go online for your images and print them off. Spend an afternoon with your partner, cutting out images and words that represent your shared dreams. Arrange them on the board and place it somewhere visible to remind you of your goals. Ours is on the wall as we walk into the kitchen. It has the next 4 years planned out. This exercise sparks creativity and opens the door to meaningful conversations about your future, helping you align your goals and build a shared vision.

Regular Check-Ins for Relationship Health

No healthy relationship runs on autopilot. It takes regular attention and effort to keep things feeling steady, supported, and connected.That's where regular check-ins come in. They're intentional conversations that help you assess the health of your relationship and address issues before they become roadblocks. Consistency is key here. Just as you wouldn't skip oil changes, you shouldn't skip these emotional tune-ups. By making them a regular part of your routine, you create a safe space for both partners to express concerns and joys. This consistency strengthens the bond and builds trust, knowing that there's a dedicated time to focus on the relationship without distractions.

To have effective check-ins, it's helpful to prepare. Think of it as setting an agenda. You might jot down key topics in advance, like emotional wellbeing or any current stressors. Scheduling is crucial too. Find a time that suits both of you, whether it's weekly or monthly. This approach ensures that check-ins don't feel rushed or forced, allowing both partners to be present. During these conversations, focus on emotional wellbeing and satisfaction. Discuss what's working and what needs attention. Address any challenges or stressors, and celebrate successes, big or small.

To get the most out of this, use positive reinforcement and appreciation. Begin with acknowledging what your partner is doing well. This sets a constructive tone and encourages open dialogue. Regular check-ins become something to look forward to, a time to reconnect and align your paths. Don't take 'I'm OK" as an affirmative all is well. Go deeper.

37 Years In, their Story:

> This couple from the Isle of Man, now 59 and 61—has been married for 37 years. They remained anonymous, but their responses paint a picture of a partnership built on longevity, mutual growth, and steady communication.

> When asked how they usually communicate, they answered with the familiar: "Pretty good, we have our moments." It's the honest, grounded reply that reflects years of shared experience.

Both partners said they "sometimes" feel truly heard, and with disagreements, they admitted that one person usually wins, but quickly added, "it works for us." There's no illusion of perfect balance here, just a dynamic that's evolved and feels right for them.

Despite differences in style, one being direct and to the point, the other more conflict-avoidant, they described their overall communication as "very similar." They talk about emotional needs occasionally and feel safe being vulnerable with each other. They haven't explored love languages, but they do know what works: "We're both good listeners."

When asked when they last felt truly connected, their answer was simple and striking: "Every day, all day." That kind of ongoing closeness isn't accidental, it's earned through consistency and a shared willingness to stay present in the relationship.

They don't point to a single breakthrough moment in how they communicate. Instead, they shared something deeper: "We've grown and evolved together, but we've communicated well from day one." After nearly four decades, that's a rare and powerful thing.

Their advice to others is as heartfelt as it is wise: "Remember that you love each other and choose your words wisely."

My thoughts:

The couple's answers reflect a long-standing connection built on respect, growth, and emotional steadiness. Their responses are simple, balanced, and powerful, especially the mix of honesty ("one of us tends to win the argument") and affection ("we feel connected every day").

Reflection Prompt:

What does "growing together" look like in your relationship? Are there habits or shared values that have helped you stay connected through different life stages?

Continuous Learning and Adaptation

Relationships are always changing, with each season bringing new challenges, insights, and opportunities to grow together. Continuous learning is the ink that keeps those stories vibrant and engaging. Relationships thrive when both partners stay informed about new communication strategies and techniques.

They breathe life into the connection, keeping both of you engaged and invested. It's about more than acquiring knowledge; it's about sharing that knowledge, experiencing growth together, and adapting to life's inevitable changes. When you approach challenges as opportunities for growth, you embrace a mindset that welcomes change. This perspective shifts obstacles from being roadblocks to stepping stones for personal and relational development.

Adopting a growth mindset means being open to feedback and ready to change, even when it feels uncomfortable. It's about recognizing that mistakes are part of learning and that every experience, good or bad, offers valuable insights. For ongoing learning, consider tapping into resources like online courses or webinars focused on relationship dynamics. Self-help books and podcasts can also provide fresh perspectives and inspire meaningful conversations. Engaging with these materials can help you both develop a deeper understanding of yourselves and each other, fostering a more resilient partnership.

Encouraging Personal Accountability

Personal accountability keeps a relationship grounded. It means owning your words, actions, and impact, without deflecting or blaming. It's about owning up to our actions and recognizing how they affect our partner. This doesn't mean blaming yourself for every hiccup, but being aware of your role and contributions. Self-awareness becomes a crucial tool here. When you're aware of your actions and their impact, you're more likely to foster trust and openness in your interactions. Accountability reduces blame and defensiveness, creating a safe space for honest dialogue. It encourages you to take a step back, reflect, and understand where you might have gone wrong, opening the door to growth and improvement.

To cultivate accountability, start by setting personal goals for your communication improvement. Maybe you want to work on listening more or being less reactive. Take a few minutes each day to jot down your thoughts on how you communicated. Were you patient? Did you listen without interrupting? These reflections provide insight into your behavior, highlighting areas for enhancement. Encouraging accountability isn't just about introspection.

Techniques for Constructive Feedback

When we think about constructive feedback, it's not just about pointing out flaws or mistakes. It's about offering observations and suggestions that help improve communication and relationship dynamics. Effective feedback is specific, balanced, and empathetic. It focuses on behaviors rather than personal attacks. It's like being a coach who wants to see the team succeed, not just a critic. In relationships, feedback plays a crucial role in fostering growth and understanding. When done right, it encourages an atmosphere of continuous improvement and openness, where both partners feel comfortable sharing and receiving insights without fear of judgment or retribution.

To deliver feedback constructively, start by using "I" statements. We covered this in chapter 4. They help express observations without blaming your partner, such as saying, "I felt unsupported when…" rather than "You never support me." This subtle shift in language can make a big difference in how the message is received. Balancing positive reinforcement with areas for improvement is also key. Acknowledge what your partner is doing well before addressing what could be better. It helps ease the tone of the conversation while reinforcing what's working, turning feedback into something you can navigate together.

Managing Stress-Induced Communication Breakdown

Have you ever felt stress creeping into your relationship like an unwelcome guest? It shows up in many forms, from financial pressures to the demands of work. These stressors don't just weigh on our minds; they seep into our conversations, affecting how we communicate. You might notice an increase in irritability or defensiveness, even in casual exchanges. It's as if stress flips a switch, turning a simple discussion into a battleground. When stress takes over, it becomes harder to listen or empathize, and misunderstandings can spiral into arguments. The key is to recognize these stress signals early and address them before they disrupt communication.

Managing stress in communication requires deliberate effort. Techniques like deep breathing and meditation can work wonders, providing a moment of calm before engaging in conversation. It's about creating mental space to approach discussions with a clear head. Setting boundaries is equally important. Protect your communication time by designating stress-free zones where you focus on each other, free from distractions and external pressures. Imagine turning off phones during dinner or scheduling a no-work-talk weekend. These minor changes can improve how you connect with your partner, opening the door to deeper connection and clarity.

Building resilience against stress is an ongoing process. Consider taking part in stress management workshops or classes together. These can offer practical tools tailored to your unique challenges. Partner relaxation sessions can also be beneficial, focusing on stress relief through activities like yoga or guided meditation. These shared experiences will help to manage stress and strengthen your bond, as you learn to support each other through difficult times. By addressing stress and its impact on your communication, you pave the way for more meaningful and harmonious interactions with your partner.

Creating Rituals for Connection

Think of rituals as the heartbeat of your relationship. They're like little anchors in the chaos of life, reminding you both of what matters. They create a rhythm and a sense of security, allowing you to reconnect and strengthen your bond regularly.

Establishing rituals doesn't have to be complex. Start by considering what activities align with both your values and interests. Maybe you both love the outdoors, so a weekend hike could be your thing. Or perhaps you're foodies at heart, so cooking a new recipe together could become your tradition. The key is to customize these rituals to reflect your shared goals and priorities. Incorporating these rituals into your daily routine can be as simple as setting aside time for a nightly chat or a weekly adventure. These intentional practices keep your relationship vibrant and connected, no matter how hectic life gets.

Brainstorming Ritual Ideas

Set some time aside with your partner for a brainstorming session. Grab a notebook and jot down activities that bring you joy. Think about what makes you both feel connected and understood. Experiment with different rituals to find what resonates. Maybe it's as simple as reading a book together or as adventurous as planning monthly road trips. This exercise sparks creativity and encourages collaboration, helping you discover meaningful ways to build connection into everyday life.

Celebrating Communication Milestones

In every relationship, communication milestones mark those pivotal moments when progress becomes tangible, like the time you finally resolved a long-standing conflict or when you noticed a significant improvement in how you listen to each other. Each milestone is a resting spot on your shared journey, a chance to soak it in, reflect, and feel proud of the path you're creating side by side. Celebrating these achievements reinforces positive behaviors, encouraging you both to continue growing and evolving together. When you take the time to celebrate, you affirm the strength of your partnership and deepen your emotional connection. This shared triumph boosts motivation, making you both eager to tackle future challenges with renewed vigor.

To celebrate these milestones, consider planning special celebrations or rewards. This could be a dinner at your favorite restaurant or as elaborate as a weekend getaway. The key is to make it meaningful and personal. Reflect on what you have learned and how far you have come.

The Future of Relationship Communication

These days, communication moves faster than ever, texts, emojis, and quick replies often replace deeper conversations. But speed doesn't always mean connection. The way we communicate in relationships is changing fast. With messaging apps, video calls, and social media, it's easier than ever to stay connected, yet sometimes these tools can make us feel more apart than together. The key is balance. Digital convenience is great, but it can't replace the warmth of face-to-face moments. The world is shifting too. There's a growing encouragement to speak more openly, to listen more deeply, and to embrace different ways of expressing love and connection.

With these changes come both challenges and opportunities. Balancing digital and in-person interactions is key to maintaining genuine connections. While technology offers ways to stay in touch, it's crucial to carve out moments for direct, personal interaction. This balance ensures that digital convenience doesn't replace the warmth of human connection. Embracing diversity in communication practices is another opportunity, allowing different voices and perspectives to enrich our interactions. Inclusivity fosters understanding and empathy, creating stronger, more resilient relationships.

To adapt to these trends, staying informed about new technologies is essential. This means taking part in ongoing education and self-improvement, keeping your skills sharp. Engaging in discussions about the evolving nature of communication can lead to innovative ideas and solutions. Imagine future relationship scenarios and plan how to adapt. This forward-thinking approach not only prepares you for changes, but also inspires creativity in maintaining strong connections. As we wrap up this chapter, keep these ideas in mind. They're not just about navigating the present, but also about building a foundation for future success in your relationships.

Conclusion

As we reach the end of this book, I hope you're not just holding a collection of strategies, but a deeper sense of confidence, clarity, and connection. Communication isn't something we master once. It's a living, breathing part of our relationships that evolves as we do. And now, with greater awareness, you get to shape it with intention.

I hope that by sharing my journey, the mistakes I've made, the patterns I've had to unlearn, the vulnerable moments when I got it wrong. You've been able to see that none of us have this figured out. It took courage for me to be open about my failed first marriage, the times I've been defensive or withdrawn, and the ongoing work my current relationship requires. But I believe there's power in honesty about our struggles. If my vulnerabilities and hard-won lessons have helped you feel less alone in your own communication challenges, then every story I've shared has been worth it.

Maybe you've already started noticing the small shifts, the pause before reacting, the courage to speak up with kindness, the power of listening. These aren't just techniques; they're love in motion.

There's no perfect way to communicate, no one-size-fits-all formula. But there is presence. There is effort. There is choosing, again and again, to meet each other with curiosity and care. That's where the magic happens.

So, as you move forward, keep asking the questions that matter. Keep showing up, even when it's hard. Keep practicing. And when you stumble (because we all do), remember: every conversation is a chance to begin again.

Thank you for letting me walk this part of your journey with you. Wherever you go from here, know that the tools are within you, and the relationship you want is always within reach.

Here's to love that listens, love that grows, and love that keeps showing up.

With gratitude and warmest wishes,

Annabel

Enjoyed This Book? Join Us in The Literary Lounge!

Dear Reader,

Thank you for purchasing [Book Title]. We hope it inspired you, taught you, and gave you plenty of moments to reflect on.

If you're looking for more great reads, insights, and a community of curious minds, we'd love to invite you to join The Literary Lounge, our FREE exclusive book club for non-fiction lovers.

As a member, you'll receive:

First access to new releases – be the first to dive into our latest non-fiction titles!

Exclusive freebies and content – enjoy monthly downloads, behind-the-scenes stories, and more.

Special book promotions – get insider tips on upcoming promotions and grab your next read for free.

Join us today and stay connected to a world of thought-provoking books, great conversations, and a community of fellow readers.

click the link to join The Literary Lounge!

Or scan the QR code

We can't wait to welcome you! Happy Reading,

The Literary Lounge Team

I hope *The Relationship Code for Couples* has given you insight, tools, and maybe even a few lightbulb moments, or laughs, along the way.

But communication isn't just something to read about, it's something to practice, live, and grow into together.

To help you keep going, don't forget to explore the free resources listed at the end of the book.

Whether it's conversation starters, reflection prompts, printable tools, or real-life case studies, these resources are here to support you beyond the final page.

If you found this book helpful, your review can make a real difference. So many couples are looking for guidance, reassurance, or just to feel less alone.

Your feedback could be the nudge they need to begin their own journey toward a stronger, more open connection.

Take a moment to leave a quick review and help more couples discover what's possible when communication truly clicks.

Click here to leave a review. Or scan on the QR code

Resources

To help you put what you've learned into action, I've created a set of free downloadable tools and exercises to support your journey.

These are simple, practical resources you can use on your own or together with your partner.

Access all resources here:

Scan Here

References & Further Reading

- Chapman, G. (n.d.). *Discover Your Love Language.* The 5 Love Languages. https://5lovelanguages.com/

- PositivePsychology.com. (n.d.). *How to Develop Empathy: 10 Best Exercises for Adults.* https://positivepsychology.com/empathy-worksheets/

- DDI. (2023). *Using Emotional Intelligence to Improve Communication.* https://www.ddiworld.com/blog/emotional-intelligence-and-communication

- Thriveworks. (n.d.). *"I" Statements: How to Use Them & Examples.* https://thriveworks.com/help-with/communication/i-statements/

- The Therapy Group of DC. (n.d.). *Effective Couples Therapy Techniques for Resolving Conflict.* https://therapygroupdc.com/therapist-dc-blog/effective-couples-therapy-techniques-for-resolving-conflicts/

- Travers, M. (2024, November 17). *The 8-Step Process of Rebuilding Trust After Cheating—By a Psychologist.* Forbes. https://www.forbes.com/sites/traversmark/2024/11/17/the-8-step-process-of-rebuilding-trust-after-cheating-by-a-psychologist/

- Epic Counseling Solutions. (n.d.). *Effective Communication Strategies for Couples.* https://epiccounselingsolutions.com/effective-communication-strategies-for-couples-a-therapists-guide/

- PositivePsychology.com. (n.d.). *21 Couples Therapy Worksheets, Questions & Activities.* https://positivepsychology.com/couples-therapy-worksheets-activities/

- Verywell Mind. (n.d.). *How to Build Trust in a Relationship, According to a Therapist.* https://www.verywellmind.com/how-to-build-trust-in-a-relationship-5207611

- Verywell Mind. (n.d.). *Mindfulness-Based Relationship Enhancement Benefits.* https://www.verywellmind.com/understanding-mindfulness-based-relationship-enhancement-4685242

- Today.com. (n.d.). *5 Apology Languages, Explained: Types and How to Find Yours.* https://www.today.com/life/relationships/apology-languages-rcna49355

- Tomova, L., & Eisenberger, N. (2019). *The Effect of Stress on Empathic Accuracy in Romantic Couples.* PubMed. https://pubmed.ncbi.nlm.nih.gov/30816779/

- Mikulin, S. (n.d.). *The Impact of Past Experiences on Current Relationships.* Medium. https://medium.com/@sheila.mikulin/the-impact-of-past-experiences-on-current-relationships-d21e978e1492

- Pangea.ai. (n.d.). *How to Communicate with Different Communication Styles.* https://pangea.ai/resources/how-to-communicate-with-different-communication-styles

- BetterHelp. (n.d.). *Strategies for Fostering Growth in a Relationship.* https://www.betterhelp.com/advice/relations/fostering-growth-in-a-relationship-key-strategies-for-success/

www.ingramcontent.com/pod-product-compliance
Lightning Source LLC
Chambersburg PA
CBHW020416080526
44584CB00014B/1362